God, Grandchildren and Golf

God, Grandchildren and Golf

Ernest R. Boisvert

Copyright © 2018 by Ernest R. Boisvert

All rights reserved. No part of this book may be reproduced, stored in a retrieval system, or transmitted in any form or by any means, electronic, mechanical, photocopying, recording or otherwise, without the prior permission of the author.

All Scripture references are from the English Standard Version unless otherwise noted.

Many thanks to David Poole whose creative ability and hard work helped bring this project to completion.

Cover Design—David Poole

ISBN-13: 978-1984957658
ISBN-10: 1984957651

Dedication

To the wonderful lady who has made it all possible:

מים רבים לא יוכלו לכבות את האהבה
Song of Solomon 8.7

Contents

FOREWORD	**9**
PART I: GOD, GRANDCHILDREN AND GOLF	**11**
1: THE FORMER GENERATIONS	**13**
2: GRANDPARENTS AND GOLF	**16**
HIT THE BALL AND DRAG CHARLIE	16
ERNEST DOMPTAIL BOISVERT	17
ERNEST WILLARD BOISVERT	19
IF I WAS A RICH MAN	23
YELLOW JACKETS	25
HAINS POINT	26
ERNEST R. BOISVERT	28
3: GOD AND GRANDCHILDREN	**40**
THE BIBLE—LEARNING ABOUT GOD	41
THE BIBLE—SEEING THE BIG PICTURE	43
DIVINE DRAMA	47
A WORD ABOUT COVENANT	50
WE WORSHIP ONE GOD IN THREE PERSONS	52
DOCTRINAL HISTORY	59
WHY BOTHER WITH HISTORY?	67
4: GOD AND THE GOSPEL	**70**
PART II: THREE MORE GS: GUILT, GRACE AND GRATITUDE	**79**
1: GUILT AND SIN	**81**
MINIMIZING SIN	83
GOLF'S HOLY GRAIL—THE HOLE-IN-ONE	92

2: Grace and Justification — 95
- The Question Lurking in Every Heart — 95
- Are We Okay? — 96
- Turning Point — 98
- Martin Luther and Justification by Grace Alone — 100
- Brush with Death — 102
- First Mass — 103
- Preaching the Bible — 105

3: Grace and Sanctification — 111
- Running the Race Set Before Us — 111
- The Finish Line — 120

4: Grace and Change — 123
- Union with Christ — 125
- We Died to Sin — 129
- Walking It Out — 131
- Clashes with Conscience — 136

5. Grace, Wisdom and the Fear of the Lord — 143
- Wisdom—The Principal Thing — 145
- Where Can Wisdom Be Found? — 146
- The Fear of the Lord — 147
- Blessed! — 151

6: Gratitude for a Grand Inheritance! — 159
- Peace with God—Reconciliation — 161
- Forgiveness of Sin — 164
- Future Inheritance—The Hope of the Resurrection — 167
- Groaning Inwardly and Waiting Eagerly — 167

One More Thing — 172
- And Glory! — 173
- Glory in Humiliation — 175

Foreword

Grandchildren are a crown of the aged. (Proverbs 17.6)

When Brit Hume was leaving as anchor of Fox News' Special Report, he was asked what he planned to do. "The three Gs," was his immediate reply, "God, granddaughters and golf." I thought, "Ah! A man after my own heart!"

This is a book about God and his ways with us. But grandchildren and golf also figure into it. When I think about my grandchildren, I wonder what they'll remember about me. Can I leave them anything of value? Right now, they're young; the oldest is just eleven. But soon they'll be grown and may wonder, "Who was that kindly old gentleman that lived with Mimi?" So, though I have a general audience in mind, my grandchildren are in the forefront of my thoughts. And as for golf, it's a thread that's wound its way throughout my entire life.

But we'll also look at another set of "Three Gs:" *Guilt*, *Grace* and *Gratitude*—concepts that undergird the Christian doctrine of redemption—God's great work of salvation. These concepts have formed the structural backbone of such historic documents as the Heidelberg Catechism.[1] Any effort taken to understand them will be repaid many times over.

---

[1] The Catechism's first question and answer captures this beautifully: "What is thy only comfort in life and in death?" "That I, with body and soul, both in life and in death, am not my own, but belong to my faithful Saviour Jesus Christ, who with his precious blood has fully satisfied for all my sins, and redeemed me from all the power of the Devil; and so preserves me that without the will of my Father in heaven not a hair can fall from my head, yea that all things must work together for my salvation. Wherefore, by his Holy Spirit He also assures me of eternal life and makes me heartily willing and ready henceforth to live unto Him." *The Heidelberg Catechism.*

PART I:

God, Grandchildren and Golf

1: The Former Generations

Remember the days of old; consider the years of many generations; ask your father and he will show you, your elders and they will tell you. (Deuteronomy 32.7)

Or, as my dad often said, "Hey, maybe the old man's not so dumb after all." Mark Twain reportedly commented, "When I was eighteen I thought my father was the most ignorant man in the world. By the time I was twenty-one I was amazed at how much the old guy had learned in three years."

But I'm suspicious of Twain. He thought golf was a good walk wasted.

Grandparents. What do you recall of your grandparents? A good deal, no doubt. And your great-grandparents? You had eight of them. Chances are you know very little. If you go back one more generation most of us would admit we know next to nothing.[1] This is a melancholy fact. It won't be long and we ourselves will be gone. A couple generations later and little trace of us will remain. Isaac Watts' lines capture this:

---

[1] "All birth, said Schelling, is from darkness into light. All origins are wrapped in obscurity. If no one tells us who our parents and grandparents are or were, we do not know it." Herman Bavinck, *Reformed Dogmatics*, Vol. 2, Baker Academic, Grand Rapids, 2004, p. 501-2.

> *Time, like an ever-rolling stream*
> *bears all its sons away*
> *They fly forgotten like a dream*
> *dies at the opening day.*[2]

The dream seemed so vivid, but upon awakening we strain to remember the details. And a few minutes later it's gone, completely gone. Will it be the same with us?

As for my own great-grandparents, I know the name of only one, Samuel Levi Willard. I know him only because he fought in the Civil War and we have his muster papers, including extensive medical records. He served with Erie Pennsylvania's 145th Infantry and saw action at Gettysburg, Spotsylvania, Wilderness, Chancellorsville, Cold Harbor, and Fredericksburg. He served under Generals McClellan, Burnside, Hooker, Meade and Hancock and was present at Appomattox when Lee surrendered. That's quite a military record.

My great-grandfather was with the Union artillery that faced Pickett as he made his famous charge. By carefully examining his records, we learned that he was suffering from bleeding hemorrhoids during the Battle of Gettysburg. He's not the only one in our family tree to deal with hemorrhoids, but good grief, right in the middle of Pickett's Charge? No battlefield glory there! His papers also indicate that many men of the 145th died at Andersonville, the notorious Confederate prison camp. Apparently, they were captured while Great-grandpa was hospitalized with his hemorrhoids. Maybe they were good for something.

---

[2] Isaac Watts, *O God, Our Help in Ages Past*, The Methodist Hymnal, The United Methodist Publishing House, Nashville, 1964, p. 28.

At some point after the war he moved to Jamestown, New York on the shores of Lake Chautauqua where he served for many years as the town sheriff. When he died at ninety-six he was one of the longest surviving Civil War veterans. Year after year Jamestown honored him by making him the grand marshal in the Memorial Day parades.

Samuel L. Willard

2: Grandparents and Golf

Hit the ball and drag Charlie

Many golfers will recognize this punchline. The guy gets home from playing and his wife asks, "Well, Dear, how was the game today?" "Terrible! Charlie had a heart attack on the second hole. And from then on it was, 'Hit the ball and drag Charlie! Hit the ball and drag Charlie!'"

This apocryphal tale (though it may have really happened) gets at an essential truth. There are those who play golf and there are golfers. Charlie and his friend were golfers.

For many years Ralph Bogart was one of the Washington D.C area's outstanding amateurs. After he died his obituary carried a comment from his wife. "When Ralph first asked me to marry him he warned me, 'You know, I'm a golfer.' I thought, 'Why should that make any difference?' Later, I found out what that meant."

There is a rough analogy with fishermen. Most of us enjoy a day's fishing but only if we actually catch something. Not the fisherman. Sure, he'd rather have a full cooler but if not, no problem. He went fishing, so it was a good day. He's a fisherman. So it is with a golfer. If the temperature is in the 30s and there's a stiff breeze, he puts on a sweater. If he's playing well or playing poorly, it doesn't matter. He's playing. And why? Because he's a golfer. It's okay if people don't understand this. We don't understand it either.

Ernest Domptail Boisvert

My grandfather was a golfer. Ernest D. Boisvert emigrated from Quebec to Bridgeport, Connecticut and married Madeline Willard. They had two boys, my dad, Ernest W. and his younger brother Richard. Grandpop Boisvert was a commercial artist who specialized in theater placards and silk screen work. According to family lore he designed the General Electric logo. This represents the high point of Boisvert fame.

I know very little of his golfing career, just a few news clippings from tournaments that he played in. Grandpop, Dad and I played together only once, a late November day in the early Sixties at Rockledge Golf Club in Hartford. That day was cold, wet and windy. We were the only ones on the course. That next summer he died. I got the news while playing at Sligo Creek. I still remember my sister running out on the course to find me. We left immediately for Bridgeport.

At the funeral, I was troubled because I wasn't crying like other family members. Then, about six months later I woke up in the middle of the night and wept deeply for him. It was my first indication of what would later help me as a pastor. Different people grieve differently—and that's okay.

Ernest D. Boisvert

Grandpop gave me my first golf club. I think I was four years old. I didn't mind that it was left-handed since I was too young to know that I was right-handed. One day my mom took me along to her china painting class at a community center adjacent to the old Indian Springs Country Club. She told me I could go outside and use my golf club.

After hacking around in the weeds for a while I noticed some grass nearby that was different—it was closely mown and smooth as a carpet. I went over to play on this nice grass and was whaling away at my ball, taking up chunks of turf when some old men came toward me, shouting. One was kinder than the others (must have been a grandfather) and explained to me that greens (whatever those are) were only for putting (whatever that was). He then sent me off to terrain more suitable for a four-year-old with a deadly weapon. Thus, I began to learn some of the game's finer points of etiquette.

Ernest Willard Boisvert

A few years later, around 1960, my father took up golf again. I say again, because he had played and caddied as a youth in Bridgeport. (One of the kids he caddied with was the smooth swinging Julius Boros. He was the Freddie Couples of his era who would win many PGA events, including three majors.) Daddy had not played golf for many years. The reason for this was World War II.

After the outbreak of the war, my father became part of the First Special Service Force. The Force was a joint United States and Canadian commando unit that saw action in the Aleutian Islands and in Europe, the only outfit to fight in both the Pacific and European theaters. Conceived by Winston Churchill for special operations, the men of the Force were paratroopers who were also equipped for mountainous and cold weather combat. A 1968 film, *The Devil's Brigade,* popularized and dramatized the Force's most famous mission, capturing a nearly impregnable Nazi mountain stronghold in central Italy. It was during this operation, the Battle of Monte la Difensa, that Dad was hit by a mortar.[1]

---

[1] Robert D. Burhans, *The First Special Service Force—A War History of The North Americans, 1942-1944*, Washington Infantry Journal Press, Washington, 1947, p. 112. The mortar also killed an officer and an enlisted man.

Uncle Richard and Dad, Bridgeport, 1943

On a macro level, wars have a way of rearranging geography. The providence of a sovereign God lies behind it all. "And he made from one man every nation of mankind to live on all the face of the earth, having determined allotted periods and the boundaries of their habitations..."[2] Often those boundary lines are redrawn through the

---

[2] Acts 17.26.

dislocations of war. What is true on a macro level is also true on a micro level. Wars have a way of redirecting individual lives.

Insignia of the First Special Service Force

WW II uprooted and relocated a young Roman Catholic of French-Canadian heritage from Connecticut to Walter Reed Army Medical Center in Washington, D.C. At the same time a Sephardic Jewish girl from Pittsburgh entered the Navy and as a first-class petty officer also came to be stationed in D.C.

Fannie Nahmod was the first of eight children born to parents who had come from Damascus, Syria. Like others of that great generation she entered the Navy willing to do anything she could to serve the war effort. But it was with reluctance that she agreed to accompany a friend going to Walter Reed one day to "cheer up the boys." Once there, she found to her horror that she was in an amputee ward. Putting her head down, she walked straight through to get out at the other end. But the ward ended in a porch where my Dad just happened to be lying. She was stuck. He engaged her in conversation and somehow made her promise to come back.

Mom -- 1945

That chance meeting led to their marriage a year later in 1945. My older sister Suzie was born in 1947 and I arrived three years later in 1950. Our first home was in N.E. Washington. Then in 1951 we moved to Silver Spring just north of the district line. A year later Joyce was born. My parents bought a small house on Georgia Avenue when it was a still a two-lane road. Today it's a major artery. About ten years later construction would begin on the Capital Beltway just a few blocks south.

Dad had lost his right leg above the knee. Shrapnel also passed through his abdomen, miraculously missing vital organs. I recall the large pits in his back where the shrapnel exited. But the most obvious thing about Dad was his wooden leg. As a little boy, I was told that this was due to the war. At first, I thought all fathers had wooden legs.

When I got a little older and realized this wasn't always the case, I reasoned that those other dads must not have gone to war. It's interesting how the limits of our experience determine our perception of reality.

I wasn't aware of any limits to Dad's abilities. Though he couldn't run he was an excellent swimmer. And when it came to fixing anything he was the guy the neighbors would always ask for. Like all small boys I thought my Dad could do anything.

Dad -- 1945

If I Was a Rich Man

Would it spoil some vast eternal plan,
if I was a wealthy man? —Reb Tevye

I am neither a rich man nor am I the son of a rich man, but we came close. Before I was born Dad enrolled in night school at Capitol Radio and Electronics Institute. This never led to a career change (he stayed with his government job at the Forest Service till he retired) but it did enable him to pursue a passion. In the late Forties he built a television set, the first in the neighborhood. Everyone would gather to watch the test pattern or the occasional Washington Capitols basketball game, at that time coached by the great Red Auerbach. There wasn't much else to see, but the future of television held great promise.

Dad was so enthusiastic about TV that he gathered together everything he could lay his hands on to invest in this new technology. In those early days there were three companies that led the way—NBC, CBS and DuMont. Ever heard of DuMont? That's where Dad put all his money.

A second opportunity for great wealth came with the stock market in the 1980s. Dad had become a fairly savvy investor turning a modest nest egg into a decent portfolio, although he was heavily leveraged. Things were booming under Reagan and the economic mood was optimistic. That is, until Black Monday in 1987. Daddy faced two margin calls within three days that wiped out just about everything. To his credit he took it philosophically, "Well, it was paper before. Now it's just less paper."

Would it spoil some vast eternal plan? Apparently, it would. But in the ways that really matter, I am a wealthy man. As the wise man of Proverbs 30.8-9 prayed:

Give me neither poverty nor riches;
feed me with the food that is needful for me,
lest I be full and deny you and say, "Who is the LORD*?"*
or lest I be poor and steal and profane
the name of my God.

Yellow Jackets

A warm summer afternoon in 1958 would become one of the worst days of my life. Dad and I were watching the Washington Senators baseball game. Mom was weeding around the azalea bushes in the front yard. Suddenly she burst through the door. "I just got stung!" she said, more angry than injured. We acknowledged and commiserated. She put some baking soda on her finger and went back out to continue weeding. But a few minutes later she came in again and this time she was crying, stung for a second time.

Dad strapped on his wooden leg, got the vacuum cleaner and went outside. I watched from a safe distance on the porch as he carefully sucked up the yellow jackets flying around the base of the azaleas. Then he dug around and uncovered their nest. He sucked that up, too. He took the bag from the vacuum and put it on a bare spot in the back yard. After pouring a little gasoline he dropped a match on the bag. We watched the flames in silence for a few moments before Dad went back inside.

I lingered with some satisfaction as the yellow jackets burned. But the bag was just barely on fire. After what they had done to mom I thought they deserved to really suffer! So, I picked up the gasoline can, walked over and started pouring. The last thing I remember was the flame climbing up the stream of gasoline before the can exploded. I was knocked backwards. It seemed the whole back yard was on fire. Soon, I heard sirens as a crowd of neighbors gathered.

Miraculously, apart from singed hair and melted sneakers, I was uninjured. But I was really scared. Not because I'd almost burned to death. That didn't even occur to me. No, what really frightened me was getting yelled at by the firemen. It seemed pretty clear that once they started asking questions, I would be in big trouble. I dreaded what was sure to come. But it never came. Nobody chewed me out. And I could never figure out why.

The answer came about forty years later. On the day that we buried Dad at Arlington National Cemetery the family gathered afterward for a meal. My sisters and I were reminiscing about childhood memories and the incident of the yellow jackets came up. When I remarked how puzzled I was that the firemen never lectured me, Suzie said, "Don't you know why? *Daddy* took the blame. He told them it was *his* fault." Her words stunned me and brought tears to my eyes. They still do. Just one of many times he sacrificed for me.

Hains Point

Around 1960 Dad bought some clubs and started playing again. He had become a cartographer with the U.S. Forest Service. Many of the guys at his office were playing golf and talking about it and Dad thought, "Hey, I can do that!" So he did, and he did it pretty well, too. He played to a nine handicap. He had enough upper body strength to hit the ball pretty far and he had a great short game.

Playing golf was the way I connected with my father. It was also my introduction in relating to adult men since he took me along to play with his buddies. Every Saturday morning starting at dawn a group of anywhere from eight to 28 men played at East Potomac Park, known to locals as Hains Point. We played year-round unless there was snow on the greens. This was pretty much a constant for me throughout junior high and high school. Learning to play in all kinds of weather gave me an edge when competing in high school and college.

With the Potomac River on one side and the Washington Channel on the other, wind was always a factor at Hains Point. The layout was completely flat and rather unimaginative. But the fairways and postage stamp greens were always in good shape for a public course. One unique feature was the huge cottonwood trees. In May when they shed their cotton it covered the greens giving the appearance of a fresh snowfall.

Dad managed handicaps for the group. He used the old USGA slide rule method to calculate them. There was always a lot of good natured griping because handicaps were the basis for all the betting that went on. But Dad always prevailed. You can't argue with math or the United States Golf Association. After the round, everybody threw a quarter into the "beer pot." The net score winner was then obligated to use his winnings to buy beer for everyone. Since I was too young to drink beer it was agreed that I could keep the pot if I won. I recall some resentment when, one year, as my game dramatically improved and my handicap went down, I walked away with the money week after week.

I enjoyed being included in this circle of men although there wasn't anything particularly deep about the interactions. I just liked being with Dad and his friends. They were the Great Depression and WW II generation, men who weren't known for being very expressive. The touchy-feely sensitive male hadn't come along yet. I'm sure they all had their cares and challenges. But the idea was to play golf, to unplug for a few hours, not to meet for deep fellowship. Looking back on these times, Thoreau's observation was probably true, "The mass of men lead lives of quiet desperation." This was certainly becoming true for me.

Ernest R. Boisvert

The "R" stands for "Robert" but I've always been known as "Robin." This confusion is due to my mom. She called me "Robin" from the beginning. I can't recall which kindergarten classmate informed me that Robin was a girl's name. I was taken aback by this news. Even though repeatedly assured that it's also a boy's name, the damage was done.

Major League baseball players like Robin Roberts and Robin Yount helped a little. Batman and Robin didn't help at all. I tried many times to shed this nickname but all my attempts were unsuccessful. Years ago, I just gave up. So, to most people, I'm Robin. For business purposes and airline tickets, I'm Ernest Robert. To my grandchildren, like a lot of other grandfathers, I'm "Pop Pop."

Names are like labels on a jar that describe the contents within whether it's apricot jelly, lima beans, woodscrews or whatever. What's in the jar is what's important. But for many years I wasn't really sure what was in my jar. I'm speaking now of spiritual matters, specifically religious identity.

Unlike today, in the Forties inter-racial marriages were almost unthinkable and, in some places, illegal. Mixed marriages, like my own parents, were merely unusual but they presented unique challenges. Like Tevye said in *Fiddler on the Roof*, "A bird may fall in love with a fish, but where will they make a home?" How about Silver Spring, Maryland?

My parents loved each other but some of Mom's family refused to accept a Gentile son-in-law. And Dad's devout Catholic mother struggled to relate to her Jewish daughter-in-law. The real issue though was how to raise the children. Dad wasn't keen on the Roman Catholic Church. His participation had been nominal at best since his youth. Mom was much more in tune with her Jewish identity.

The bird and the fish came up with an uneasy truce. Our family would believe in God but would not formally join any religious community. We would celebrate both Chanukah and Christmas. Whether this description is completely accurate or not, it's what got through to me. As a child, I understood very little of this.

In 1956, Mom took me to see a blockbuster film starring Charlton Heston, "The Ten Commandments." Before entering the theater, she bent down and said earnestly, "I want you to know, this really happened." Those words made a lasting impression on me.

It was great to get presents for Christmas *and* Chanukah. But whenever the topic of religion came up among friends or classmates, I was uncertain and uncomfortable. It didn't help matters when Mom told me that if I had lived in Europe during WWII they would have killed me. "Why!?" "Because you're Jewish." I know now that she only wanted to instill in me some sense of identity, but at the time, she only succeeded in scaring me. Gosh, if that's the case, I don't want to be Jewish. So, I grew up confused about religion, not knowing if I was Jew or Gentile, fish or fowl—or what. I knew these things were important, but beyond that I was clueless.

In my young mind, however, there was someone who rose above all the confusion. That was Jesus. Although I knew next to nothing about him, I somehow sensed he was good in a way similar perhaps to George Washington or Abraham Lincoln. What fascinated me about Jesus was his connection with the cross. Two blocks up Georgia Avenue was the local Catholic Church, St. John the Evangelist. On the front of the church was a mosaic of the crucifixion scene. The bus stop across the street faced it. I often sat on the bench waiting for the bus and puzzling over that scene. If he was good, why did he die like that? What did it mean?

I stumbled and bumbled my way through Montgomery Hills Junior High and Albert Einstein High School, surviving the seemingly endless teenage years of pimples and braces. I wanted to play baseball or football but wasn't big enough or good enough. So, even though it wasn't cool I kept playing golf and eventually became team captain.

1968

We weren't very good. Most of the high school teams in Montgomery County were filled with well-to-do country club kids who'd benefited from lessons and unlimited opportunities to play. In my whole time at Einstein I think we had just three kids from clubs.

Things changed when I got to Montgomery Junior College. We were very good. MJC had never lost a head to head match. In my first year, we won the state and regional tournaments and travelled to Roswell, New Mexico for the nationals, where we finished in twelfth place. The next year we went to the national tournament again, this time in Miami, but didn't do quite as well. I was playing to a five handicap at the time. I was also regularly stoned.

I been in the right place
But it must have been the wrong time
I'd of said the right thing
But I must have used the wrong line[3]

It was the late Sixties, and the times, they were a-changing. By my second year at MJC, I was fully involved in the counter-culture. Virtually every societal institution was coming under scathing critique. The country was involved in an unpopular war and young people like myself were in full-throated protest.

Drugs were an important part of the protest. I started smoking marijuana the summer after graduating from high school. The thing about pot (weed, for those in the 21st century.) is that it deceives you into thinking you're smarter than you are. Since I was a highly functioning pothead, I was fooled into taking a *mañana* attitude toward every area of

---

[3] Dr. John the Night Tripper, *Right Place, Wrong Time*, 1973. Dr. John's way of expressing the universal truth that humankind is fundamentally out of sync with its Creator, something I felt acutely at this time.

life, including my academic work. *Mañana! Not today. I'll get to it tomorrow.*

I was in an engineering program and my second-year studies required calculus and physics. It seems incredible to me now, but I actually thought I could get by without buying the textbooks! Up to that point, I'd never really had to study to succeed. Things had come easily.

My life interests consisted only in playing golf and getting high, so school was pretty much an afterthought. It was while at the national tournament that I decided to call home and tell Dad about the good round I'd just shot. He didn't want to hear it. His words were clipped, "Robin, your grades just came in the mail. This is ridiculous!"

That spring semester I failed two four-credit courses. My grade point average nosedived. Dad had been paying my tuition and was understandably displeased. I wish I could say that was the low point, but there would be many points much lower over the next two years.

Eventually I dropped out of school, left home and floundered around in different jobs. But I didn't give up weed. For the next two years I contrived to get high and stay high in various ways. It was a lifestyle. But the highs weren't very high anymore and without some mood-altering substance, life was a drag.

Today I wonder about a culture pressing for legalization of marijuana. I understand the argument for decriminalizing it, but do we really need more people rolling stoned? There's a reason we called it "dope."

Reflecting back on this period I wasn't trying to give anybody a hard time, especially my dad. And I was unaware how my indolence was affecting others. As I began to reap more of what I had sown, I grew depressed and hopeless.

The trajectory of my life was downward. I became reclusive withdrawing from friends and normal activities.

Was I going crazy? *One Flew Over the Cuckoo's Nest*, Ken Kesey's novel about life in a mental institution, was trendy at the time. I feared that was where I was headed. The words of Deuteronomy Chapter 28 described me well. "Night and day you shall be in dread and have no assurance of your life. In the morning you shall say, 'If only it were evening!' and in the evening you shall say, 'If only it were morning!' because of the dread your heart shall feel...." Those were dark, dark days.

Eventually I got a job as a maintenance man at a nursing home. There I met a girl who invited me to go with her to a Roman Catholic folk mass at George Washington University. It was the church's attempt to appeal to a younger crowd. I was more interested in the girl than the folk mass. I agreed to go. We'd get stoned on the way downtown.

I was okay with the church service. It was sincere and I found it somewhat comforting. But the real turning point came with a family we met there. Joe and June were a middle-aged couple living in Manassas, Virginia. Joe was crew cut and worked for IBM. Not very hip. But they were friendly and took an interest in us, often inviting us to their home for lunch.

As I got to know them, I became more and more impressed. It was clear that he loved his wife and that she respected him. Their children (all six) obeyed them and they were happy, *joyfully happy*! I was attracted to them and strangely affected by them. Sunday afternoons at their home became the high point of my week.

33

But they were *very* religious, at least that's how I saw it. It was "praise the Lord" for this and "praise the Lord" for that. I found out later they were charismatic Catholics. They believed in the present-day activity of the Holy Spirit including his gifts—healings, miracles, tongues, prophecy, the whole deal. With no religious background I had no categories for any of this.

* * *

I had recently started reading the Bible. I'd never read it before. I read hoping to find some comfort but It didn't comfort me. Rather, it upset me. I had started reading Genesis in the Old Testament. But when I got to the stories of Jacob and Esau, I didn't like God choosing one over the other. It didn't seem fair to me. I was unaware that while I was busy judging God, God was judging me. I hit a brick wall in my Bible reading.

Then someone suggested I try reading the New Testament. I read the four gospel accounts of Jesus, beginning with Matthew. Ah! This thrilled me. The Jesus that I had wondered about years earlier came alive as I read about his miracles and marveled at his teachings. At the end of each gospel story, Jesus was crucified. But then he rose from the dead! Amazing. So this is what Christians believe?! Okay, I'm officially interested.

I continued reading the fifth book of the New Testament, *The Acts of the Apostles*. This fascinating narrative of the first believers after Jesus held my attention. After a few chapters, the story focused on a character named Saul who persecuted the early Christians. While he was on his way to Damascus to arrest some of them, he supposedly had an experience that turned him into a Christian. Then he changed his name to Paul and started writing letters telling people what to do.

Yeah, right. I had a problem with that. First of all, people don't just change like that. Second, Paul was only a man. So, who was he to tell others how to live? At this point my agreement with Christianity was about at the level of *The Byrds* who sang, "Jesus is just all right with me." I'm okay with Jesus, but this guy, Paul? Sorry. That's asking way too much.

I was aware of a difference between myself and people who identified as Christians. I sort of believed in Jesus and was kind of prepared to say that he's all right, which I considered to be quite radical. But apparently more was needed. Jesus' own words challenged me. "If anyone would come after me, let him deny himself and take up his cross and follow me. For whoever would save his life will lose it, but whoever loses his life for my sake will find it."[4]

Evidently, following Jesus would require something more so I began to do a cost analysis. I had yet to realize just how much it would cost to obey God. Intuitively, I knew that my lifestyle would have to change. But in my superficial thinking, I thought it only meant the drinking, smoking and drugs would have to go. And yes, I also sensed that it would cost me socially. Christians and Christianity was *not* considered cool. My friends were already worried I was becoming a Jesus freak.

I was in a car with some of those friends when one of them cracked a joke mocking Jesus. Everyone laughed but me. Uh-oh. A moment of truth had arrived. "Hey, Boisvert. What's with you? You don't believe this Jesus crap, do

---

[4] Matthew 16.34-35.

you?" After an awkward pause I weakly replied, "Uh, yeah. I guess so." Embarrassed silence followed. Everyone sensed this was serious. It wasn't exactly *Profiles in Courage*, but I recall it now as my first real profession of faith.

What do you think of Jesus? That's a question everyone must reckon with.

> "Who do people say that the Son of Man is?" And they said, "Some say, John the Baptist, others say Elijah, and others Jeremiah or one of the prophets." He said to them, "But who do you say that I am?" Simon Peter replied, "You are the Christ, the Son of the living God."[5]

Who do *you* say that Jesus is? If he is the Son of God, the implications are enormous.

* * *

March 5, 1972 was a dismal Sunday afternoon. My mood fit the weather. I was at a friend's house getting ready to take him to the airport. Weary with life, I wondered, how long is this going to go on?

The only ray of hope seemed to lie in the direction of Jesus but I didn't know what to do or how to proceed. I was more anxious than usual, very ill at ease. I went into the bathroom just to get a moment alone. It was there that I prayed as sincere and desperate a prayer as I had ever uttered, perhaps my first true prayer. "God, if you are real,

---

[5] Matthew 16.13-16.

Jesus, if you are real, please help me! I don't want to do any more drugs or alcohol or cigarettes."

The only problems I could see at this point were my obvious bad habits. I was clueless as to the true nature and depth of my plight—alienation from God. But my prayer was sincere. My error was in thinking that being a Christian was entirely a matter of my own effort.

After that prayer, I determined I would try my best to be a Christian, which to me meant no drugs, drinking or smoking. So I gathered up all the will power I could muster to steer clear of these things. I wasn't sure how long I could hold out but I would give it my best. Monday, Tuesday and Wednesday— I was hanging in and hanging on, operating on sheer willpower. Then I decided to pull out all the stops. I would fast; that's what really religious people did! So, Thursday, Friday and Saturday, no food!

Then came Sunday and a prayer meeting at Joe and June's home in Manassas. After a welcome meal, they prayed with me to be filled with the Holy Spirit. I felt a pleasant sense of peace and well-being but nothing dramatic. I returned home to Takoma Park.

But something had changed. The next day avoiding my bad habits didn't seem to require the same level of effort. I could live without them. I became vaguely aware of something different, what I now know to be God's help, the help of his Spirit. This was all very new to me. I was still shaky but the Bible was making more sense.

In particular, John Chapter 14 became precious to me. Here, Jesus spoke to his disciples about fear and promised the Holy Spirit would come to comfort them. "Let not your hearts be troubled, you believe in God, believe also in me."[6]

---

[6] John 14.1 (KJV).

It was a personal invitation from Jesus to trust him. I was so moved by this that I memorized the entire chapter. Nobody told me to do it and it wasn't a chore, it was a joy. It was truth believed and applied. Yes, things were definitely changing.

* * *

Probably the most amazing thing about this period was something that I didn't even realize at first. But a little background is necessary. A couple of years earlier, on a Thursday night in May, I was at a rock concert at Montgomery Junior College. Someone offered me a tab of LSD. I had never tried it before and since I am rather cautious, I cut the tablet in half. After a few minutes when it seemed like nothing was happening, I took the other half. Later I learned that it was a four-hit tab of "purple flash."

That evening I began an acid trip that increased in intensity over the next twenty-four hours and took me into the stratosphere. At first things were cool but after a while I knew it was more than I could handle. By this time, I was back at home watching the Johnny Carson show with my mother and trying to hold myself together. Johnny was doing some strange things before my eyes. I called a friend and told him what was happening. He brought me to his home and cared for me for the duration of the trip. I am still grateful for his kindness.

I seemed to teeter on the cliff's edge of insanity for many hours. Somehow, I managed not to fall off but the aftereffect was deep-rooted anxiety. Virtually every day for the next two years I would experience periods of heavy sighing accompanied by fear. How close was I now to the edge? I was never sure. Mentally, I was a very shaky guy.

But one evening a few weeks after my experience with the Holy Spirit as I was washing the dishes, it dawned on me. I haven't felt afraid! I haven't felt that sighing and fear! For how long? I traced it back and realized it had been since that prayer meeting. God had powerfully yet imperceptibly removed the nasty monkey that had been on my back for two years! Wow, *that* was power!

> *My chains fell off, my heart was free; I rose, went forth, and followed Thee.*[7]

While it wouldn't be true to say I've never felt fear since, I have found Someone who is greater than all my fears, Someone who met my deepest needs. As Jesus said to his disciples on that scary Thursday night before he was crucified, "Let not your hearts be troubled. You believe in God, believe also in me."[8]

---

[7] Charles Wesley, *And Can It Be That I Should Gain*, The Methodist Hymnal, Nashville, 1964, p. 527.
[8] John 14.1.

3: God and Grandchildren

Why can't I see God; Is he watching me?
Is he somewhere out in space, or is he here with me?
I am just a child; teach me from his word;
then I'll go and tell to all the great things I have heard.
Teach me while my heart is tender,
tell me all that I should know,
And even through the years I will remember,
no matter where I go.[1]

At the time of this writing my fourteen grandchildren range from eleven months to eleven years. I'm sixty-eight.

---

[1] Judy Rogers, "Why Can't I See God?" *Songs on the Westminster Catechism*, www.judyrogers.com, 1991.

Sociologists label this "early old age." Luther, Calvin and Spurgeon were gone before they reached sixty. I have been a pastor for over forty years, and though the following reflections may sound like pastoral memoirs, I'm really only trying to answer a question for my grandchildren: "Who was Pop Pop and what did he think was important?"

The Bible—Learning about God

J.I. Packer commented in a recent interview that while we live in a science-oriented culture where people demand objective proof, they still have a deep-seated sense that God exists and want to know Him. "The secret," Packer insists, "is learning from the Bible. It's all there, and God has put it there for us to instruct us about how we are to think of Him and how we are to relate to Him. He's told us what He has done, what He is doing and will do."[2]

When I was twenty a friend asked me if I believed the Bible. I replied, "The Bible was written by men, men make mistakes, therefore the Bible is full of mistakes." I hadn't really thought it through. I was just repeating what I heard someone else say. I wonder how often we do that.

My friend was disappointed by my answer but on my twenty-first birthday, she gave me a Bible anyway. Secretly, I was delighted. I read it hoping to find comfort for my troubled soul but the result was mounting *dis*comfort.

A year later, after repenting of my sin, believing the gospel and receiving the Holy Spirit, my attitude toward the Bible changed completely. That's because the same Spirit

---

[2] *Knowing the Reality of Our Triune God,* byfaithonline.com/knowing-the-reality-of-our-triune-god; June 2017.

now living in me[3] had also inspired and directed the human authors of Scripture so that they wrote exactly what God wanted to them to write. "All Scripture is breathed out by God,"[4] Paul told Timothy. He was referring to the writings of the Old Testament, but the same is true for the New Testament. The Bible is entirely reliable since it comes from God. It is God's written revelation of himself. And the reason he gave it to us is that he wants to become friends with us, a truly delightful thought!

Not all parts of the Bible are easily understandable. Some are quite difficult. But overall the message of Scripture is clear and open to those who read it with the intention of obeying God. Part of my problem when I first began was my attitude toward the Bible's Author. It was anything but humble. God will give grace to the humble, but he resists the proud.[5] And when God resists you, you go nowhere.

Growing spiritually requires spiritual food. The Bible is food for our souls. The prophet Jeremiah said, "Thy words were found and I did eat them and thy word was unto me the joy and rejoicing of my heart."[6] Jesus said, "Man shall not live by bread alone, but by every word that proceeds from the mouth of God."[7] Spiritual growth is simply impossible without reading and reflecting upon the Bible.

I once counseled a man who was discouraged and depressed. When I asked how long he'd been like this, he guessed it had been about six weeks. Then I asked him about his relationship with God, in particular Bible reading

---

[3] Romans 8.11, 15-16; Galatians 4.6.
[4] 2 Timothy 3.16a.
[5] I Peter 5.5b.
[6] Jeremiah 15.16 (KJV).
[7] Matthew 4.4; Luke 4.4.

and prayer. He told me, "Honestly, I've been too discouraged to read the Bible." "For how long?" "About six weeks." A faint smile crept over his face as he made the connection. I'm not implying solutions to our problems are simplistic. But *the* major element in spiritual well-being is relating closely to God. And hearing from his Spirit through his Word is the primary way this happens.

Don't be lazy about this. Read your Bible. Read it today. Read it every day. Read those parts that are familiar and comforting. But in addition, read it through from beginning to end for that will force you to read parts that are unfamiliar and challenging. And when you've read it all the way through, go back to the beginning and start again. This has been my habit for the last 45 years. I can't think of any other one thing that has served me so well.[8]

The Bible—Seeing the Big Picture

The Bible is a big book containing different kinds of writings. While it may not be apparent at first, there is a theme running through Scripture that ties it all together. It is possible to trace a plotline that moves through the various books of the Bible, both Old and New Testaments. This unifying thread is actually a unifying person.

At the end of Luke's Gospel, a fascinating exchange occurs between Jesus, who just hours before had risen from the dead, and two despondent disciples.

> That very day two of them were going to a village named Emmaus, about seven miles from Jerusalem,

---

[8] A good study Bible is a worthwhile and necessary investment. The NIV and ESV translations have fine study Bibles.

and they were talking with each other about all these things that had happened. While they were talking and discussing together, Jesus himself drew near and went with them. But their eyes were kept from recognizing him. And he said to them, "What is this conversation that you are holding with each other as you walk?" And they stood still, looking sad. Then one of them, named Cleopas, answered him, "Are you the only visitor to Jerusalem who does not know the things that have happened there in these days?" And he said to them, "What things?" And they said to him, "Concerning Jesus of Nazareth, a man who was a prophet mighty in deed and word before God and all the people, and how our chief priests and rulers delivered him up to be condemned to death and crucified him. But we had hoped that he was the one to redeem Israel. Yes, and besides all this, it is now the third day since these things happened. Moreover, some women of our company amazed us. They were at the tomb early in the morning and when they did not find his body they came back saying that they had even seen a vision of angels who said that he was alive."

And he said to them, "O foolish ones, and slow of heart to believe all that the prophets have spoken! Was it not necessary that the Christ should suffer these things and enter into his glory?" *And beginning with Moses and all the Prophets, he interpreted to them in all the Scriptures the things concerning himself.*[9]

Here, Jesus withholds his identity and feigns ignorance in order to engage these two disciples on his own terms. After listening, he reproves them for being slow to grasp

---

[9] Luke 24.13-23, 25-26, (emphasis added).

that what had happened was absolutely necessary. Then he takes them on a tour of the Scriptures, interpreting it all as concerning himself. A few hours later, when Jesus appeared to the eleven disciples, he does the same thing.

> These are the words that I spoke to you while I was still with you, that everything written about me in the Law of Moses and the Prophets and Psalms must be fulfilled.[10]

In these conversations, Jesus makes it clear that all the categories of Old Testament Scripture—Law, Prophets and Writings—are about him. Jesus Christ himself is the focus of all Scripture. It's all about him. He then goes on to say:

> Thus it is written, that the Christ should suffer and on the third day rise from the dead, and that repentance and forgiveness of sins should be proclaimed in his name to all nations, beginning from Jerusalem. You are witnesses of these things.[11]

It's about him, but it is *for us, for our salvation*. The reason Jesus suffered and died was for our redemption! This good news of forgiveness is now being proclaimed to all nations. The gospel message has traveled around the world and down through the centuries as faithful witnesses have proclaimed its truth. The fruit of this message and the manifold wisdom of God is now evident in the church of Jesus Christ.[12]

---

[10] Luke 24.44 (emphasis added).
[11] Luke 24.46-48.
[12] Ephesians 3.10, 21.

Theologians use the term *redemptive history*[13] to describe the person and work of Jesus Christ. It started before his incarnation. Moses and the prophets wrote of him. He's there in the Psalms, as well. Therefore, with Christ as the key it is possible to go back and unlock the Bible to see how it unfolds the drama of redemption.

* * *

The Bible presents history from a redemptive perspective, giving us God's take on it. Every historian chooses what he will include and what he will leave out. His decisions reflect his worldview. Scripture gives us God's worldview, what he considers important. Most of the Bible is written in the genre of historical narrative, i.e. in story form.

From the beginning God is clearly the chief actor. He created the heavens and the earth and everything in them, things both visible and invisible. He created it all out of nothing (*ex nihilo*)[14] so there is a clear distinction between God and his creation. That means that if all creation ceased to exist, God would still exist for only he is eternal and self-existent.

Everything God created was good. He created man (both male and female) in his image to have fellowship with him and serve as his vice-regents over creation. In this regard, he gave the man and the woman a task. They were

---

[13] Or *salvation history*.

[14] This Latin term for "out of nothing," means God did not use any pre-existing material in creating the heavens and the earth. Before creation all that existed was the triune God—Father, Son and Holy Spirit.

to be fruitful and multiply, to fill the earth and manage it for him. He also gave them a command, "You may surely eat of every tree of the garden, but of the tree of the knowledge of good and evil you shall not eat, for in the day that you eat of it you shall surely die."[15]

But they disobeyed his command and punishment followed. Sin entered into the world and death resulted as the consequence of sin.[16] God confronted the man and woman over their sin, but he also immediately began to act on their behalf. He spoke to the serpent and said, "I will put enmity (hostility) between you and the woman and between your offspring and her offspring; he shall bruise your head and you shall bruise his heel."[17] It's important to see that God took the initiative in this.

These words predict a conflict of cosmic proportions. Although obscure at first, this conflict becomes increasingly clear as redemptive history progresses. It finds its highest expression as Jesus, offspring of the virgin's womb, crushes the serpent through his death on the cross and subsequent resurrection.[18]

Divine Drama

The story of the Bible has been described as a drama in three acts—*creation*, *fall* and *redemption*.[19] The first three chapters of Genesis give us Acts I and II, creation and fall.

---

[15] Genesis 2.16-17.
[16] Romans 5.12.
[17] Genesis 3.15.
[18] Romans 16.20; I John 3.8b.
[19] Some add a fourth—glory. Cf. Thomas Boston, *Human Nature in its Four-Fold State*, C. Brightly and Co., Bungay, 1812.

The rest of the Bible sets forth Act III, redemption—the story of God's mighty works to reclaim fallen man from his terrible plight.

A key point in the drama occurs when God speaks to Abraham in Genesis 12. God's words to him are of the utmost importance for understanding the Bible's message. At this time, Abraham was merely a wandering Aramean,[20] no different from anyone else in the ancient world.

> Now the LORD said to Abram, 'Go from your country and your kindred and your father's house to the land that I will show you. And I will make of you a great nation, and I will bless you and make your name great, so that you will be a blessing. I will bless those who bless you, and him who dishonors you I will curse, and in you all the families of the earth will be blessed.'[21]

This magnificent promise marks the beginning of a *covenant* God made with Abram. He said he would make from him a great nation, but a nation requires at least two things: people and land.[22] At this point Abram had neither. He was childless and his wife was barren. As for land, he was told only that he must go from his own country to a land that God would show him.

This must have seemed very sketchy, for even the writer of Hebrews states, "And Abraham went out, not knowing where he was going."[23] It may have been a grand

---

[20] Deuteronomy 26.5.
[21] Genesis 12.1-3. His name would later be changed to Abraham.
[22] Law and leadership (a king) are also necessary and will come in due time.
[23] Hebrews 11.8b.

promise but it was unclear and undefined. Following these instructions would require faith, not blind faith but a settled trust in God's actual words.

In time, a promised miracle child, Isaac, was born to Abraham and his formerly barren wife, Sarah. Then Isaac begat Jacob and Jacob the twelve patriarchs. Four hundred years later, by the time of Moses, Abraham's descendants had greatly multiplied but were living as slaves in Egypt.[24] Never in a hurry, God continued to move deliberately, fulfilling his plan and keeping his promise.

Under Moses the deliverer, God brought his people out of Egypt and into the land he had promised to Abraham many years before. At Sinai, the covenant relationship with God's people was further clarified and developed.[25] This is the substance of Exodus, the second book of the Bible.

After entering the land of Canaan and dispossessing its inhabitants, the nation of Israel eventually came to be led by kings. The greatest of these was David and under his leadership the nation prospered. God made a further covenant with David promising that of his descendants he would always have a son who would reign in a perpetual kingship.[26]

God's relational purpose in making these covenants with his people can be seen in the oft-repeated words, "And I will be your God and you shall be my people."[27]

---

[24] Exodus 1.7, 9-12, 20.
[25] Exodus 20 ff. The covenant was codified as the law of Moses.
[26] 2 Samuel 7.
[27] E.g. Jeremiah 30.22.

A Word about Covenant

The covenant agreement was common in the Ancient Near East.[28] When a great king (suzerain) entered into a covenant with a lesser king (vassal) they followed a somewhat standard procedure. The formal covenant began with a preamble and then a prologue describing the history of their relationship. Following this, the terms of the covenant were stated. Then came a list of the blessings that would result from obedience and the curses for disobedience. Often an animal was cut in two and the participants would walk between the parts, symbolizing the fate of the covenant breaker. It was all capped off with a sacrificial meal.

If the covenant's terms were broken, the great king would send a representative, a royal emissary to speak in his name. This representative would remind the lesser king of what he had promised and how he had broken the covenant. A warning would follow and if there was no change, punishment would be carried out.

This summarizes the role of the Hebrew prophet. Like a royal emissary the prophet would speak in the name of the Great King, Yahweh, and like a prosecuting attorney he would remind Israel of the covenant laws, warning them of the judgment that would result if there was no change.

Israel refused to listen to her prophets although God sent them repeatedly. Finally, due to disobedience over a long period, Israel experienced the ultimate curse, exile from the land. The northern tribes were taken captive by

---

[28] Cf. Meredith G. Kline, *The Structure of Biblical Authority*, Wipf & Stock Publishers, Eugene, 1989.

Assyria in 721 BC. and a century later, the southern kingdom of Judah was carried off by Babylon.

Following a seventy-year exile, the captives began to return, first under Zerubbabel and then under Ezra and Nehemiah. The Jewish people were re-established in their land but were greatly diminished. God was still with his chastened people, however. He again sent prophets to encourage their faint hearts. The last of these was Malachi around 450 BC.

The prophets were not only prosecuting attorneys for the law of Moses. They were also heralds of the Abrahamic covenant of grace.[29] The most important feature of God's promise to Abraham was that *through him all the families of the earth would be blessed*. This covenant of grace was to be extended to the Gentile nations of the world.

Although Jesus Christ (son of Abraham, son of David[30]) was sent to the lost sheep of the house of Israel,[31] he always had the Gentile nations in view.[32] God's promise to Abraham was fulfilled in Jesus. Through Jesus' gospel the blessing of Abraham comes to Gentiles as well as Jews. Paul addressed mainly Gentile believers in Galatia (present day Turkey) saying:

> And the Scripture, foreseeing that God would justify the Gentiles by faith, preached the gospel beforehand to Abraham, saying, 'In you shall all the nations be blessed,'... so that in Christ Jesus the blessing of Abraham might come to the Gentiles, so

---

[29] The Covenant of Moses was also gracious, but served a more specific purpose for the nation of Israel in its time.
[30] Matthew 1.1.
[31] Matthew 15.24.
[32] Luke 4.25-27.

that we might receive the promised Spirit through faith.... Now the promises were made to Abraham and his offspring. It does not say, 'And to offsprings,' referring to many, but referring to one, 'And to your offspring,' who is Christ. ... For in Christ Jesus you are all sons of God through faith.... And if you are Christ's then you are Abraham's offspring, heirs according to promise.[33]

I have been accused by dispensationalist[34] friends of preaching "replacement theology," the idea that a Gentile church has replaced God's people Israel. But if anything, this is "inclusion theology," the gracious message that through faith in the gospel the door of salvation has opened to include Gentiles as well as Jews.[35]

This is made abundantly clear in Paul's Letter to the Ephesians where the Gentiles who were once strangers to the covenants of promise have been brought near by the blood of Christ and the dividing wall that separated Jew from Gentile has been broken down by Jesus so that the two might be made one people of God.[36]

We Worship One God in Three Persons

I was standing in line at a McDonalds in 1972. Recently born again, I was as excited as a person could be about his

---

[33] Galatians 3.8, 14, 16, 26-29.
[34] For an irenic critique of dispensational theology, cf. Vern Poythress, *Understanding Dispensationalism*, P&R, Phillipsburg, 1987.
[35] Cf. the excellent treatment of the themes of covenant and Israel by O. Palmer Robertson in *The Christ of the Covenants* and *The Israel of God*, P&R Publishing, Phillipsburg.
[36] Ephesians 2.11-16.

new-found faith. The two ladies behind me were having an animated discussion about something in the Bible. They were loud enough that I felt comfortable in turning around to say with a smile, "Hi, I'm a Christian, too."

Instead of returning my smile, the one lady cast a sideward glance, "Do you believe in the Trinity?"

"Uhh, yeah!"

"Well, it's not in the Bible!" And with that she turned back to her prior conversation.

That was my first indication that we all don't see this the same way. They were Jehovah's Witnesses[37] although I didn't know that at the time. As a matter of fact, the lady was correct in what she said. The word *Trinity* does not occur in the Bible. It is a combination of the ideas of three and one, a theological term, a shorthand way to denote the deepest of mysteries—one God in three Persons. It is a helpful term, and while it may not occur in the Bible, what it represents most certainly does!

Of the Trinity, Augustine wrote, "In no other subject is error more dangerous, or inquiry more laborious, or discovery of truth more profitable."[38] The doctrine of the Trinity is difficult because it requires diligent examination of Scripture in a serious and sustained manner. It is dangerous because heresy looms on every side. But John Frame, agreeing with Augustine, says, "The study can seem

---

[37] The most notable feature of this group is its refusal to acknowledge the divinity of Jesus Christ, Son of God. Cf. Bruce M. Metzger, *The Jehovah's Witnesses and Jesus Christ: A Biblical and Theological Appraisal*, Theology Today, 1953, pages 65-85.

[38] St. Augustine, *De Trinitate*, Trans. Edmund Hill, O.P., New City Press, Hyde Park, 1991, p. 68.

technical and dry, but the rewards are great."[39] Any effort expended in understanding this is worthwhile because *this is who God is*.

We ought to desire to know God as he has revealed himself. We cannot love whom we do not know. But is it really practical to try to understand a mystery so deep? Consider Ferguson's observation about Jesus' final words to his disciples on the night before his death:

> I've often reflected on the rather obvious thought that when his disciples were about to have the world collapse in on them, our Lord spent so much time in the Upper Room speaking to them about the mystery of the Trinity. If anything could underline the necessity of Trinitarianism for practical Christianity, that must surely be it.[40]

The one true God has eternally existed as Father, Son and Holy Spirit. The Father is God, the Son is God, the Holy Spirit is God *and* there is one God. This is not a contradiction. To say that he is one God and three Gods would be a contradiction. Or to say God is three persons and one person would also be a contradiction. But to say God exists eternally as Father, Son and Holy Spirit *and* each person is God *and* there is one God, is no contradiction.

The Westminster Shorter Catechism presents this in questions 5 and 6:

---

[39] John Frame, *The Doctrine of God*, P&R Publishing, Phillipsburg, 2002, p. 621.
[40] Sinclair Ferguson, quoted by Robert Letham, *The Holy Trinity*, P&R Publishing, Phillipsburg, 2004, p. 1.

Are there more Gods than one? There is but one only, the living and true God.

> How many persons are there in the Godhead? There are three persons in the Godhead: The Father, the Son and the Holy Spirit, and these three are one God, the same in substance, equal in power and glory.

The preceding paragraphs are statements regarding the *doctrine* of the Trinity. The Trinity has of course always existed. The doctrine or teaching about the Trinity, however was progressively revealed in Scripture and hammered out in the early centuries of the church. This doctrine was present but *concealed* in the Old Testament Scriptures. It was *revealed* in the New Testament writings. And it was *formulated* in the history of the early church.

> The Old Testament contains in seed form what is more fully made known in the New Testament. On that basis, we may reread the Old Testament, just as we might reread the early chapters of a detective mystery, looking for clues that we missed the first time, but now are given fresh meaning by our knowledge of what comes later.... The original readers would not have grasped this, but we, with the full plot disclosed, can revisit the passage and see the clues there.[41]

To begin with, the tone of the Old Testament is strongly and clearly monotheistic. "Hear O Israel: The LORD our God, the LORD is one."[42] This is because prevailing religious

---

[41] Ibid, Letham, p. 20.
[42] Deuteronomy 6.4.

notions in the ancient world were all polytheistic and attended by idolatry. God, strongly opposed to idolatry, wanted his people Israel to stand apart from it in stark contrast. That is why the character of the Old Testament is monotheistic. Clues about the Trinity are there but are difficult to discern.

As one example, in Exodus 3.2-6 Moses meets a mysterious figure, the "angel of the LORD." He is then identified with God yet somehow distinct from him. No explanation for this puzzling arrangement is given.

> And <u>the angel of the LORD</u> appeared to him in a flame of fire <u>out of the midst of a bush</u>. He looked, and behold, the bush was burning, yet it was not consumed. And Moses said, "I will turn aside to see this great sight, why the bush is not burned." When the LORD saw that he turned aside to see, <u>God called to him out of the bush</u>, "Moses, Moses!" And he said, "Here I am." Then he said, "Do not come near; take your sandals off your feet, for the place on which you are standing is holy ground." And he said, "I am the God of your father, the God of Abraham, the God of Isaac, and the God of Jacob. And Moses hid his face, for he was afraid to look at God.

Similar occurrences may be noted in Genesis 16.7-13; 21.17-18; Judges 2.1-5; 6.11-24, etc. In Isaiah 63.7-14 the LORD, the angel of the LORD and the Holy Spirit are all named. Many other "clues" could be cited together with corresponding references from the New Testament that throw light back on them. B.B. Warfield summed up the OT testimony to the Trinity with an elegant analogy:

> The Old Testament may be likened to a chamber richly furnished but dimly lit; the introduction of light brings into it nothing which was not in it before; but it brings out into clearer view much of what is in it but was only dimly or even not at all perceived before. The mystery of the Trinity is not revealed in the Old Testament revelation; but the mystery of the Trinity underlies the Old Testament revelation, and here and there almost comes into view. Thus, the Old Testament revelation of God is not corrected by the fuller revelation which follows it, but only perfected, extended and enlarged.[43]

With the advent of Jesus Christ, the Son of God, a new dimension in the revelation of God comes into view. It was clear to the NT Church that Jesus was to be worshipped. "In the beginning was the Word and the Word was with God and the Word was God…. And the Word became flesh and dwelt among us."[44]

Jesus came to reveal the Father, to make him known.[45] In John Chapters 13-17 he refers to God as his Father more than forty times.[46] This was revolutionary. There are but few references to God as Father in the Old Testament, but with the coming of Jesus this changes dramatically. *Father* is shown to be God's personal name in relation to Jesus, revealing a degree of intimacy never before seen.

Jesus' own divinity is abundantly attested to in the New Testament. Occasionally you will hear someone say, "Jesus never said, 'I am God.'" Although this is technically correct,

---

[43] B.B. Warfield, *Biblical Doctrines*, Oxford University Press, New York, 1929, pages 141-42. Cf. Letham, p. 32.
[44] John 1.1, 14; 20.28 appear as bookends declaring Christ's divinity.
[45] John 17.3; Matthew 11.27.
[46] The Gospel of John uses *Father* 122 times.

it hardly refutes the overwhelming evidence.[47] Similarly, the Holy Spirit is divine and personal. A number of triadic statements in Scripture place Father and Son and Spirit together on the same plane of divinity. The most familiar of these is Jesus' great commission statement at the end of Matthew's Gospel.

> All authority in heaven and on earth has been given to me. Go therefore and make disciples of all nations, baptizing them in the name of the Father and of the Son and of the Holy Spirit, teaching them to observe all that I have commanded you. And behold, I am with you always, to the end of the age.[48]

Here Jesus refers to the *name* (singular) of the Father, the Son and the Holy Spirit. Baptisms occurred frequently in the church. Each time this happened these words were repeated and the church was reminded again of the trinitarian nature of God.

How did they understand this? More specifically, how did the first Christian believers (who were all Jews) go from Jewish monotheism to Christian trinitarianism without falling into pagan polytheism? This is the question that *required* the theological formulation of the doctrine of the Trinity.[49]

---

[47] Cf. any systematic theology, e.g. Grudem, Berkhof, Reymond, Frame, Erikson, Hodge, etc.

[48] Matthew 28.18-20.

[49] Some say, "We don't need theology. It only divides people. The important thing is to just love Jesus!" But that immediately prompts the question, "Who is Jesus?" E. g. to 'just love the Jesus of the Jehovah's Witnesses,' is in fact to deny him. We can't avoid theology. Whenever we reflect on Scripture, we are doing theology. Cf. Wayne

Doctrinal History

The early church faced challenges on two fronts: persecution from the outside and heresy from within. Jesus had warned of them.[50] Paul also predicted that erroneous and heretical notions would arise.[51] The development of sound doctrine was a safeguard against this.

Doctrinal development is a necessary part of Christian faith and tradition. Believers reflect on Scripture to rightly understand it in order to worship and serve God faithfully. The challenge in this case was to harmonize what appeared to be incompatible, how God could be one and also three. The central question was the precise nature of the relationship between the Father and the Son. This came to a head in the 4th Century.

At opposite ends of the spectrum were the errors of *subordinationism* and *modalism*. As the word would indicate, *subordinationism* viewed the Son (and the Holy Spirit) as *less than* or *inferior to* the Father in status or being. The motivation was to guard against the charge of tritheism, the belief in more than one God. But the problem was that this view robbed the Son and the Spirit of their full divinity, something clearly taught in the Bible.

Modalism, on the other hand, blurred the lines of distinction between Father, Son and Spirit, implying the one God merely has different modes or manners of expression. This preserved the oneness (unity) of God, but did so at the expense of any real distinctions among the members of the

---

Grudem, *Systematic Theology*, Zondervan, Grand Rapids, 1994, pages 26-37.
[50] E.g. John 16.1-4; Matthew 7.15-20.
[51] Acts 20.30; I Corinthians 11.19.

Godhead. It therefore threatened the possibility of having true knowledge of God. (Modalism is the error expressed in the analogy that the Trinity is like H_2O, which can appear in gas, liquid or solid forms.)

The controversy erupted when a presbyter named Arius[52] challenged his bishop, Alexander of Alexandria (Egypt), who had been teaching on the unity of the Godhead. Arius accused Alexander of a form of modalism. But Arius himself asserted that the Son of God was created and not eternal, the subordinationist error.[53]

Factions developed around differing points of view. Some held with Arius that the Son was *inferior* to the Father. Another party saw the Son as *similar* in substance to the Father. But what eventually came to be recognized as the orthodox view understood the Son to be of the *same* substance as the Father. The church father Athanasius (whose name fittingly rhymes with tenacious) consistently maintained this latter position. Christ's death for our sins required that he be fully divine as well as fully human. In other words, our very salvation depends upon an accurate understanding of the nature of the Son of God and the Trinity. The stakes in this could not have been higher!

In the unfolding controversy, which covered most of the 4th Century, many discreditable things happened that would make sensitive Christians wince. Politics and personal differences, as well theological ones entered into the debate. The Roman Emperor Constantine asserted his

---

[52] The Arian Controversy (c. 318) takes its name from him. He eventually drops from the scene, contributing little more than his name to the debate of the following decades. Present day Jehovah Witnesses' doctrine of Christ closely resembles the Arian position.

[53] R.P.C. Hanson, *The Search for the Christian Doctrine of God*, Baker Academic, Grand Rapids, 1988, p. 6.

authority when he summoned a council to be held at Nicea in 325 AD. There is no doubt that he was interested in the unity of the empire for the sake of stability. But virtually everyone, from Constantine down to the Alexandrian dock workers, was paying close attention to the truth issues at stake.

From this council a statement was produced that would eventually become known as the Nicene Creed, stating that Jesus Christ was of the same divine nature as the Father, very God of very God.

The preceding portrayal passes over much that is important in a truly fascinating drama.[54] The result of Nicea (further developed and reaffirmed at the Council of Constantinople in 381) has been the unchanging and secure possession of the church ever since, whether Roman Catholic, Eastern Orthodox or Protestant. It is hard to overstate the importance of this. This beautiful statement of the doctrine of God rewards prayerful consideration. It protects the full divinity and full humanity of our Lord Jesus Christ.

The Nicene Creed:

> We believe in one God, the Father, almighty, maker of heaven and earth, of all things visible and invisible;
> And in one Lord Jesus Christ, the only-begotten Son of God, begotten from the Father before all ages, light from light, true God from true God, begotten not made, of one substance with the Father, through

---

[54] For a fuller discussion see Davidson, *A Public* Faith, <u>The Baker History of the Church, Volume 2</u>, Baker Books, Grand Rapids, 2005, pages 19-100. For an exhaustive appraisal, cf. Hanson.

Whom all things came into existence, Who because of us men and because of our salvation came down from heaven, and was incarnate from the Holy Spirit and the Virgin Mary and became man, and was crucified for us under Pontius Pilate, and suffered and was buried, and rose again on the third day according to the Scriptures and ascended to heaven, and sits on the right hand of the Father, and will come again with glory to judge the living and the dead, of Whose kingdom there will be no end;

And in the Holy Spirit, the Lord and life-giver, Who proceeds from the Father, who with the Father and the Son is together worshipped and together glorified, Who spoke through the prophets; in one holy Catholic[55] and apostolic Church. We confess one baptism to the remission of sins; we look forward to the resurrection of the dead and the life of the world to come. Amen.[56]

* * *

Theologians have found it helpful to consider the Trinity from two complementary perspectives:

---

[55] *Catholic*, as used here, denotes the universal nature of the church, not *Roman Catholic* as understood today.
[56] The Niceno-Constantinopolitan Creed, J.N.D. Kelly, *Early Christian Creeds*, Longman, New York, 1960, p. 297-98. Besides being an edifying statement of belief, an important benefit of the creed is its ability to fence out error. Of course, reciting a creed does not make one a Christian. But presumably, anyone committed to error would be unable to recite it.

1. *The Ontological Trinity* (also known as the Immanent Trinity) is a view of the Trinity considered in itself and refers to the eternal relationships of the three Persons. The Greek word *ontos* denotes the substance, essence or being of God, that is, his deity. Each Person of the Trinity has the same being, the same *ontos*. In terms of relationship, we can say with Scripture that the Son is eternally begotten of the Father and the Father eternally generates the Son and the Holy Spirit eternally proceeds from the Father and the Son. In these particular ways they are distinct.

2. *The Economic Trinity* (also known as the Functional Trinity) refers to the activity of the Triune God in creation and redemption. In this sense, the distinctions of role help us understand how the three Persons function together. They do not all have the same roles. The Son died on the cross, not the Father. The Father sent the Son, not the other way around. Here, the Son is willingly subordinate to the Father in that he always obeys the Father and does that which pleases him. But this in no way implies that the Son is inferior to the Father since he remains at all times equally divine and of the same substance as the Father and the Spirit.

These are not two different trinities, but the same viewed from different perspectives. They may be distinguished but never separated.[57]

---

[57] I advance the following with hesitation, since a complementarian position regarding the marriage relationship is better served by the

One of the difficulties of trying to understand heavenly things is the limitation of earthly language. This is particularly true when trying to speak of the Trinity, the deepest of mysteries. We know we cannot explain the Trinity or plumb its depths. We may go only so far as Scripture allows. Yet the tradition of the doctrine's discussion has made use of extra-biblical words to aid the conversation. There is nothing inherently wrong with this as long as we recognize the limitations.

For example, the word *person* when referring to the *Persons* of the Trinity cannot be thought of in the same way that we ordinarily use the word.[58] For humankind, each

---

analogy of Christ and the Church, as Paul demonstrates in Ephesians 5. Nevertheless, there is a rough analogy in marriage that with care, may help us think about this. My wife and I are of the same being (*ontos*), we are both human beings, created in the image of God (Genesis 1.27). We are also joint heirs of the grace of life (I Peter 3.7), equally important in God's eyes. But viewed functionally we have different roles and we are not fully interchangeable parts (Ephesians 5.22-33.). We are, at the same time, both alike and different. Failure to distinguish just how we are alike and how we are different will lead to confusion and frustration in our marriage. From an ontological view we are the same, but functionally we are different—husbands and wives have different roles. Thankfully, God has revealed his wisdom on the marriage relationship in Scripture. Cf. two excellent recent books on the marriage relationship: Tim Keller, *The Meaning of Marriage*, Dutton, New York, 2011; Ray Ortlund, *Marriage and the Mystery of the Gospel*, Crossway, Wheaton, 2016.

[58] A large part of the difficulty the early church faced was the way the Greek and Latin speaking participants understood the words being used. "These differences in language and terminology, Augustine says, must be seen in context, as referring to a reality greater than human language or thought can encompass. We must use terms—from the necessity of speaking—while recognizing that they refer to things that

person is a completely separate entity. When used of God though, each *Person* indwells the others and shares the identical divine substance.[59] Why then do we use the word *Person*? As someone has said, it's because we prefer to say something rather than nothing.

The same principle applies to analogies that have attempted to explain the Trinity. They all fall short. When I was teaching on this a few years ago, I mentioned that the ice, liquid, gas analogy was the ancient modalistic heresy, Sabellianism. A home schooling mom almost fell out of her chair! However (and I hope I was able to reassure her), though all natural analogies are defective, they do no harm as long as we understand they can at best only shed light on some aspect of the Trinity and never fully explain it. We are in the deepest of deep waters here. This is who God is.

Robert Letham has stimulated my thinking and worship of our Triune God. I fully agree with his assessment that a recovery of appreciation for the Trinity will revitalize the church's life and witness.[60] The inter-trinitarian love that has been eternally expressed among Father, Son and Spirit in turn encourages us to love God and our neighbors.

Islam, by comparison, perceives God as absolutely one (monad). Relating to him is primarily a matter of submission to his will. The Christian also submits to God but his motivation for this is born out of love for the God who is eternally loving in himself and eternally giving of himself. He demonstrated this by loving us so much that he gave us his Son. May all praise be to him: Father, Son and Holy Spirit.

---

cannot be uttered, for God is more truly thought than uttered and exists more truly than he is thought." [Letham, p. 192]
[59] Letham, op. cit., p. 6.
[60] Ibid, pages 7-13.

Perhaps the best way to conclude this is with a magnificent statement from an ancient father. Gregory of Nazianzus was one of the three Cappadocians[61] and a key figure in the formulation of the Nicene-Constantinopolitan Creed. He wrote the following:

> This I give you to share, and to defend all your life, the one Godhead and power, found in the three in unity, and comprising the three separately; not unequal, in substances or natures, neither increased nor diminished by superiorities or inferiorities; in every respect equal, in every respect the same; just as the beauty and the greatness of the heavens is one; the infinite conjunction of the three infinite ones, each God when considered in himself; as the Father, so the Son; as the Son, so the Holy Spirit; the three one God when contemplated together; each God because consubstantial; one God because of the monarchia. No sooner do I conceive of the one than I am illumined by the splendor of the three; no sooner do I distinguish them than I am carried back to the one. When I think of any one of the three I think of him as the whole, and my eyes are filled, and the greater part of what I am thinking escapes me. I cannot grasp the greatness of that one so as to attribute a greater greatness to the rest. When I contemplate the three together, I see but one torch, and cannot divide or measure out the undivided light.[62]

---

[61] The Cappadocian Fathers, Gregory of Nyssa, Gregory of Nazianzus and Basil the Great figured prominently in the final phase of the Trinitarian crisis. Cf. Letham, pages 146-166.
[62] St. Gregory of Nazianzus, Letham, op. cit., p. 164.

Why Bother with History?

Ask the former generation and find out what their ancestors learned.[63]

Why? Because history has to do with memory and personal identity resides in memory. So, if you don't know your history, you don't know who you are.

One staple feature of situation comedy has been the character who sustains some trauma—a blow to the head—and suffers amnesia. His first question is always, "Who am I?" Loss of memory equals loss of identity. Our understanding of ourselves as individuals is tied to the knowledge of our personal history. We know who we are by knowing where we've been.

What is true for individuals is also true for nations, cultures, religions and the Christian Church. Without a knowledge of our history we lack identity—we don't fully know who we are. We lack content and we lack context. We become vulnerable. So, those who write history control a great deal. It's not too much to say that, humanly speaking, whoever controls our understanding of the past controls our future.

---

[63] Job 8.8 (NIV).

The Little Man Who Wasn't There

These photos show Josef Stalin, leader of the former Soviet Union (1929-1953) inspecting the White Sea Canal with some of his officials. On his right are Voroshilov and Molotov (yes, the cocktail is named after him). On his left is Nikolai Yezhof. This little man (5'0") was head of the NKVD

(Stalin's secret police) during the deadliest period of The Great Purge (1936-1938). Up to 1.2 million Russians were arrested, tortured and executed under his reign of terror. This included many artists, authors, scientists and non-political persons. After presiding over these enormities, Yezhof himself fell out of favor and was executed for anti-Soviet crimes.

If Stalin decided someone had become a liability, that someone simply disappeared and in many cases, was removed from official photographs—literally airbrushed out of history. It was said, "Everywhere else it's impossible to predict the future but in the Soviet Union it's impossible to predict the past."[64]

Crass attempts to control minds by re-writing history still occur. But those who engage in serious historical study are less likely to be fooled, are in a stronger position to understand the present and therefore wisely engage the future. In a word, they know who they are. Study history!

---

[64] Charles Krauthammer, freebeacon.com/.../krauthammer-shreds-state-departments-commitment-transparency, June 1, 2016.

4: God and the Gospel

The gospel is the most important message in the world and the only essential message in the world.[1]

What is the gospel? The word means "good news." Right. But what *is* that good news? It's the central message of the Christian faith. Okay, but just what *is* that message?

I have often asked this question and received a variety of responses, most of which have been wide of the mark. Before going on, try to answer the question yourself. *What is the gospel?*

For the first months of my Christian life I could not have given a clear answer. This came home to me shortly after my conversion. I was eager to talk about God to anyone who would listen. One afternoon I picked up a hitchhiker on Nebraska Avenue. When I began telling him how Jesus had changed my life, his eyes got really big. Then he announced, "I too have received light!" As it turned out, his light had come through a then-popular guru. He considered me his spiritual brother since "it mattered not through whom the light had come."

"Daggone it!" I thought. I knew what I had was different but I had no way of convincing him. It was becoming clear to me that my experience was in need of better explanation. I was driven by this and similar episodes to learn and appreciate the biblical and historical bases of

---

[1] Jerry Bridges, "Gifts of Grace to Build the Church," sermon preached at Covenant Life Church, Gaithersburg, November 23, 2008.

the gospel. Both the hitchhiker and I had had religious experiences, but mine conformed to the objective facts of the history of Jesus Christ—the gospel.

The first thing to recognize is that the gospel is not something done *by* us (that would not be good news), but a proclamation of something that has already been done *for* us. God has taken the decisive first step by giving his Son.

A brief but faithful definition of the gospel is, "God... gave his one and only Son." (John 3.16) Another brief but accurate statement is, "Christ died for our sins; Christ rose from the dead." Our Christian faith begins not with something we must do, but something he has done. It remains for us to discover just what it is that he has done and what it all means, so that we may honor God by believing it.

The content of the gospel is Jesus Christ himself. It consists of his holy history—his eternal pre-existence, virgin birth, holy life, atoning death, bodily resurrection and ascension and future return in glory.

It may help to describe the gospel in terms of other things closely associated with it but distinct from it. Consider the familiar verse, John 3.16, phrase by phrase:

God so loved the world	This is the motive for the gospel—God's love.
that he gave his only begotten Son	This phrase captures the gospel itself.
that whoever believes in him	Faith must be our response to the gospel.
should not perish, but have eternal life	Consequences follow rejection or belief.

In a specific place and at a specific time, Jesus Christ entered this world.

> But when the fullness of time had come, God sent forth his Son, born of woman, born under the law, to redeem those under the law, so that we might receive adoption as sons.[2]

Christ's entrance into the world was also in accord with Scripture, God's written revelation.

> Now I would remind you, brothers, of *the gospel* I preached to you, which you received, in which you stand, and by which you are being saved, if you hold fast to the word I preached to you—unless you believed in vain.
> For I delivered to you as of first importance what I also received: that Christ died for our sins *in accordance with the Scriptures*, that he was buried, that he was raised on the third day *in accordance with the Scriptures*, and that he appeared to Cephas (Peter) then to the twelve....[3]

"The Scriptures" refer to the writings of the Old Testament. The gospel is not an innovation without connection to God's past revelation. It is clearly displayed in the pages of the New Testament, but was witnessed to by the Law and the Prophets of the Old Testament.[4] As mentioned earlier, the testimony of all Scripture is *about* Jesus Christ and it is *for* our redemption.[5]

---

[2] Galatians 4.4-5.
[3] I Corinthians 15.1-5 (emphasis added).
[4] Romans 3.21.
[5] Luke 24.44-47.

What do the Scriptures teach us about this unique individual, Jesus Christ? First, we learn of His eternal pre-existence. Jesus became incarnate in the fullness of time. We celebrate his birth every Christmas. But this Son of God, this Second Person of the Trinity has always existed.

> "In the beginning was the Word and the Word was with God and the Word was God. He was in the beginning with God. All things were made through him and without him was not anything made that was made…. And the Word became flesh and dwelt among us and we have seen his glory…"[6]

> "But you, O Bethlehem Ephrathah, who are too little to be among the clans of Judah, from you shall come forth for me one who is to be ruler in Israel, whose origin is from of old, from ancient days."[7]

He is the only person whose human nature was conceived by a miracle of the Holy Spirit. Born of a virgin, he went on to live the only sinless human life the world has ever known. Jesus Christ is fully human and fully divine.

It is just here that virtually every cult goes wrong, denying Jesus Christ when they reject his full divinity, sinlessness or virgin birth. Of course, these are great mysteries. But to deny any of them is to deny Christ. Mary was understandably perplexed when she asked the angel, "How can this be…?" She was simply told, "Nothing is impossible with God." And that was good enough for her.[8] Let us follow her example.

---

[6] John 1.1-3, 14.
[7] Micah 5.2.
[8] Luke 1.34, 37-38.

Jesus lived a sinless life in perfect obedience to the will of his Father. In doing so, he fulfilled all righteousness for our sake.[9] The very righteousness of Jesus Christ becomes ours through union with him by faith. His holy life culminated in his atoning death on the cross.

That cross is the heart of the gospel. For Paul, there was nothing more central or profound. "I resolved to know nothing among you except Jesus Christ and him crucified."[10] It is important to realize that the cross was the perfect will of God. It was not that an unfortunate set of political circumstances led to Jesus' demise. No, his crucifixion was according to the predetermined counsel and foreknowledge of God. His death was not a failure of mission but a fulfillment of God's perfect will.[11]

Jesus' death was both *substitutionary* and *sacrificial*. This means he took our place and died to pay the penalty for our sins. The best way to consider these terms is to look back to their origin in the Old Testament sacrificial system. In it, God demonstrated that sin is so serious it must be atoned for. An Israelite bringing a sin offering would lay his hand upon the animal's head. This would demonstrate the transference of his guilt onto the innocent animal which was then slaughtered and placed on the Lord's altar. The animal was the sinning man's *substitute* and was *sacrificed* in his place.

In this example, a man takes a lamb for himself. At the Passover, it would be a lamb for a household. On the Day of Atonement, a lamb was taken for the nation. But when John

---

[9] Matthew 3.15; Philippians 3.9.
[10] I Corinthians 2.2.
[11] Acts 2.23.

the Baptist saw Jesus he said, "Behold the Lamb of God who takes away the sin of the world!"[12]

Furthermore, Jesus' death satisfied the righteous anger of God.[13] The idea that God has anger is jarring to modern ears but unless we reckon with it we can neither appreciate the gospel nor be faithful to Scripture.

The wrath of a just and righteous God is essential to his being. God would be deficient in character if he were not angry with evil and sin. By suffering on the cross, Jesus *propitiated* (turned away) God's fearful wrath for those who trust in him, turning that wrath into favor.

But it was because of God's love that he gave his son. And it was due to Jesus' love that he gave his life. The cross therefore demonstrates *at the same time* the justice of God and the love of God.

It is impossible to fully appreciate the amazing grace of our loving God if we are not aware of our desperate condition apart from Jesus Christ. His death by itself does not show us the love of God. It is his death *for our sin*.

> If I'm sitting quietly on a pier in the sunshine enjoying the day and someone jumps into the water and drowns shouting 'I love you,' I do not really see the point. But if I'm caught in a raging torrent and someone at the risk of his life jumps in to save me, then I can speak of a revelation of love.[14]

---

[12] John 1.29.
[13] This "satisfaction theory" of the atonement has been the dominant understanding of Christ's death in most of the Protestant Church.
[14] Leon Morris, *Glory in the Cross*, Baker Book House, Grand Rapids, 1966, p. 62.

After Jesus died and was buried, he rose from the dead. The resurrection is essential to the gospel. Paul stated it as a matter of fact and as a matter of first importance in his letter to the Corinthians.[15] This is not an optional doctrine. It is the Father's way of saying, "I accept the sacrifice of my Son as payment for the penalty of sin." He was raised for our justification, vindicating the Father's justice.[16]

Jesus triumphed over death as well as sin and holds out to us the guarantee of life beyond the grave.[17] In spite of the skepticism of a faithless age, the church today sustains the same Easter testimony of our ancient forefathers confessing, "He is risen. He is risen, indeed!"

And if he is risen, he is alive. In fact, he ever lives to make intercession for us.[18] A few weeks after his resurrection, Jesus astonished his disciples by ascending bodily in their full view.[19] He then sat down at the right hand of the Father and from that position of authority, sent the Holy Spirit to fill believers and empower the church for her mission. Jesus Christ continues to sit in session as head of the church and Lord of every individual Christian until the time comes when he will return in glory.[20]

All this Jesus has done and will do. He did it all in obedience to the Father. It was done especially for us but without our asking, without us even realizing our need. It was done for us while were his enemies![21] This is a gospel that is gracious from start to finish. It is perfect and

---

[15] I Corinthians 15.3-4.
[16] Romans 3.25-26; 4.25.
[17] I Corinthians 15.20-23.
[18] Hebrews 7.25.
[19] Acts 1.9-11.
[20] Mark 8.38; Luke 9.26; 2 Timothy 4.1.
[21] Romans 5.6-10.

complete. It never needs to be repeated and it cannot be added to. It is full, finished and final!

And it is all a matter of historical record. When these truths about this person are known and trusted, they provide the only sure foundation for a life of satisfying service to the true and living God. Basing our faith not on ourselves, our efforts or our feelings but on what he alone has done, we are then able to serve him freely. And this we do, not to gain his acceptance but because we already have it. Now *that* is good news! How I wish I'd been able to tell this to my hitchhiker friend that day. Who knows? Perhaps we'll meet again.

PART II:

Three More Gs:

Guilt, Grace and Gratitude

1: *Guilt* and Sin

Toward the end of his life, Karl Menninger, considered by many the dean of American psychiatry, wrote a book with a provocative title, *Whatever Became of Sin.* In it he noted that the word "sin" and the concept it represented began to disappear from our culture around the middle of the twentieth century.

> In all of the laments and reproaches made by our seers and prophets, one misses any mention of 'sin,' a word which used to be a veritable watchword of prophets. It was a word in everyone's mind, but now rarely if ever heard. Does that mean that no sin is involved in all our troubles—sin with an 'I' in the middle? Is no one any longer guilty of anything? Guilty perhaps of a sin that could be repented or repaired or atoned for? Is it only that someone may be stupid or sick or criminal—or asleep? Wrong things are being done, we know; tares are being sown in the wheat field at night. But is no one responsible; is no one answerable for these acts? Anxiety and depression we all acknowledge, and even vague guilt feelings; but has no one committed any sins? ... The very word 'sin,' which seems to have disappeared, was a proud word. It was once a strong word, an ominous and serious word. It described a central point in every civilized human being's life plan and life style. But the word went away. It has almost disappeared—the word, along with the notion. Why?

Doesn't anyone sin anymore? Doesn't anyone believe in sin?[1]

Menninger should be applauded for pointing this out. But most people would still say the greatest problem afflicting us is just plain ignorance. "If people were better educated, if they could see the bigger picture, better understand other cultures, then there wouldn't be all these difficulties," they might tell you. "More education would eliminate racism and the misunderstandings that separate people. Education and training would enable the poor to get better jobs and avoid drugs and crime."

There is obviously truth in this. But there is a more fundamental problem and Menninger hints at it. A moral model of understanding human responsibilities and problems has all but been replaced by a scientific medical model, so that those who commit heinous crimes are rarely referred to as wicked or evil or sinful, but as sick, mentally ill, those whose brain chemistry has gone awry.

Menninger's appeal to reconsider sin as a culprit is a step in the right direction, but upon closer examination, even his view is inadequate. That is because he sees sin on an entirely horizontal level, the sin of one person against another or perhaps against oneself. But to fully comprehend the nature of sin we must recognize its vertical dimension: that sin is primarily an *offense toward God*.

Psalm 51 vividly expresses this. Here David pours out his heart to God in repentance. He had previously been outwardly rebuked by the prophet Nathan and inwardly convicted by the Holy Spirit for his sin against Bathsheba

---

[1] Karl Menninger, *Whatever Became of Sin?* Bantam Books, New York, 1973, pp. 15-16.

and her husband Uriah. Yet, in spite of what he had done to them, he cries out to God, "Against you, you only have I sinned and done what is evil in your sight."[2] David was not denying his sin against Bathsheba and Uriah, but he was acknowledging the fundamental character of every sin, regardless of its type: it is against God.

Sin—what an unpleasant subject! And a difficult one, besides. But it is absolutely essential to consider, because if our understanding of it is deficient, so will be our knowledge of the Father, Jesus, the Holy Spirit, the law of God, the gospel and the way of salvation. An accurate understanding of sin is the bottom button on the shirt of redemptive theology. If it's in the wrong buttonhole, the whole shirt is askew.

Minimizing Sin

Minimizing sin is as common as sin itself. The fact is, we always give ourselves the benefit of the doubt. If really pressed we may refer to our sin as a "weakness" or "shortcoming" or "error in judgment." But sin is not a minor issue. If there is no sin, there is no point in talking about salvation from sin. If it's no big deal, why did Jesus have to die? The matter is complicated further by the fact that sin affects our very thinking about the subject. Left to ourselves we can't come to clear views of it. But thankfully God has given us his infallible word on it.

The early chapters of Genesis spell out humanity's sinful dilemma. And Romans 3.23 declares that all have sinned and fall short of the glory of God. It is universal. It is

---

[2] Psalm 51.4.

a powerful force opposed to God, so strong and overwhelming that only one Person has ever been free from it.

Sin is the transgression of the law.[3] Any failure to conform to the moral will of God as revealed in Scripture, not just in action, but also in thought and inclination, is sin. God gave the law which reflects his holy character. He stands behind it. And when we break God's laws he takes it personally.

A famous passage in Isaiah captures the self-centered nature of sin.

> All we like sheep have gone astray; we have turned each one to his own way; and the LORD has laid on him the iniquity of us all.[4]

We are like sheep, the least intelligent of barnyard animals. We are prone to wander. Each of us turns to his own way. This is the heart of the matter, living our lives without reference to the God who created and sustains us. Though we may not state it quite so bluntly, Henley's lines express it well.

> *It matters not how strait the gate,*
> *How charged with punishments the scroll;*
> *I am the master of my fate,*
> *I am the captain of my soul.*[5]

The scope of sin is so great that the Bible uses many different words and figures to convey its appalling nature

---

[3] I John 3.4.
[4] Isaiah 53.6.
[5] William Ernest Henley, *Invictus*, Bartlett's Familiar Quotations, Little, Brown, and Company, New York, 1919, p. 829.

and disastrous effects. Wrapped up in that one little word are the ideas of rebellion, transgression, wickedness, confusion, shame, unfaithfulness, lawlessness, ignorance, disobedience, perversion, evil and more.

Anyone reading the first chapters of Paul's letter to the Roman Christians is struck by his withering appraisal of the entire human race. Both Jew and Gentile are locked up in the bondage of sin. Paul's words are so forceful and unequivocal that our tendency is to regard him as reasoning in the extreme. "Hey, he must be talking about Hitler or Jack the Ripper!" But he's not. He's talking about all of us, himself included. "There is none righteous, no not one.... There is no one who does good... all have sinned...."[6]

Part of our problem in understanding this is that we tend to evaluate ourselves in relation to others. So, compared to Attila the Hun, I'm doing well. Compared to Mother Teresa, maybe not so much. But God doesn't grade on the curve. And unless he reveals to us, we cannot discern the depths of our depravity.

In the 1980s I lived in the beautiful farm country of Lancaster, Pennsylvania. Life there was pleasant in all respects but one: I could never get used to the smell of manure. Pig manure was by far the worst. But though I found their smell disgusting, the pigs didn't seem to mind. "The very animals whose smell is most offensive to us have no idea they are offensive and are not offensive to one another."[7]

What is the source or origin of this sin problem? Paul explains it in the fifth chapter of Romans (verses 12-21).

---

[6] Romans 3.10, 12, 23.
[7] J.C. Ryle, *Holiness*, Evangelical Press, Hertfordshire, England, 1979, p. 65.

(Note that this discussion of sin pertains to man's natural state apart from grace. Through Christ's redemptive work, man's relationship to sin has been radically changed. Stay tuned!)

Sin came upon all men because of the sin of one man—Adam. This is proven by the fact that all men die, with physical death as the punishment for sin. This is known as the doctrine of original or inherited sin. When I was a junior in high school, we studied the Puritan era in American History. My text book had an illustration of an elementary reading primer used by the Puritans. It said the following: "In Adam's fall, we sinned all." I was offended by that. I remember thinking, *"It's just wrong to brainwash children like that!"* Then, thinking more in terms of myself, I really got upset. *"I don't see why I should be dragged down by Adam. After all, I don't know him from Adam!"* To say I had a problem with this doctrine would be an understatement. And I'm not alone. It offends our sense of fairness. The natural man finds it abhorrent.

But Paul's point in describing our inherited and inherent sinfulness is not to irritate us. It is to inform us. Understanding our relationship to Adam is key to understanding our relationship with Jesus Christ. In fact, these two, Adam and Christ, are representative heads of the human race with regard to the economy of redemption. Romans 5.11-21 is an extended comparison and contrast of the two men and their effect on mankind.

The great twentieth century English preacher, David Martyn Lloyd-Jones wrote, "If you ask me, 'Is it fair that I be counted sinful because of the sin of Adam?' I will reply by asking, 'Is it fair that you be counted righteous because of the righteousness of Christ?'"[8]

Sin is the universal inheritance handed down from our common father, Adam. It renders us guilty before God and antagonistic toward him. This teaching directly contradicts the idea that we enter the world with a blank slate, a *tabula rasa*, as the philosopher David Hume contended.

As a result, although man continues to bear God's image, that image has been defaced. He is now like the ruins of an ancient Greek temple. The marks of grandeur are still evident, but the glory is departed. Like a mirror cracked, God's image remains but is largely distorted.

Two further aspects of this inheritance are:

- **Pervasive (total) depravity**—this indicates that sin's corruption affects man in every part of his being: his mind, his emotions, his will, his body. Nothing in him is left unaffected by sin.

- **Total inability**—this does not mean that man is unable to do any good by *human* standards. He can and does perform good deeds and may possess many fine qualities. But in regard to spiritual things, he is powerless. And even the "good" things he does are tainted by sin. As the Westminster Confession has it, "having fallen into sin, man has completely lost his ability to do anything to contribute to his salvation."[9] Apart from Christ, nothing that a man does can please God because he is neither

---

[8] D. Martyn Lloyd-Jones, Romans: Assurance, Chapter Five, Zondervan Publishing House, Grand Rapids, 1972, p. 219.
[9] Westminster Confession 9.3.

motivated by God's grace nor concerned for God's glory. And God is supremely concerned with our motives and his glory.

Jeremiah affirms this inability when he asks, "Can the Ethiopian change his skin or the leopard its spots? Neither can you do good who are accustomed to doing evil."[10] When Paul told the Ephesians that they had been *dead* in their trespasses and sins, he was helping them understand not only God's overwhelming grace in saving them, but also their absolute need for that grace. There is nothing a dead person can do to contribute to his salvation.

> He who looks upon sin merely as a fiction, as a misfortune, or as a trifle, sees no necessity either for deep repentance or a great atonement. He who sees no sin in himself will feel no need of a Saviour. He who is conscious of no evil at work in his heart, will desire no change of nature. He who regards sin as a slight affair will think a few tears or an outward reformation ample satisfaction. The truth is no man ever thought himself a greater sinner before God than he really was. Nor was any man ever more distressed at his sin than he had just cause to be.[11]

Perhaps we can agree with this assessment when thinking about sin before conversion. But what is the effect of sin after conversion? Is it no longer present? The presence of sin still remains, but its power over the Christian is broken. Romans chapter six makes that clear

---

[10] Jeremiah 13.23.
[11] William S. Plumer, *The Grace of Christ*, Presbyterian Board of Publication, Philadelphia, 1853, p. 24.

enough. Its presence is still a factor, but our relationship to it has been radically altered.

The Holy Spirit dwells within the believer showing us the way to walk with God and giving us the power to do so. We are no longer under sin's domination. It no longer has the authority to enslave us. The threat of judgment due to sin no longer hangs over us. Yet sin's influence still dogs our steps.

One helpful way to understand this is by considering three different time tenses Scripture uses to describe our relationship to sin: We *have been delivered* from the **penalty** of sin; we *are being delivered* from the **power** of sin; we *shall be delivered* from the **presence** of sin.

Nevertheless, as counterintuitive as it sounds, the closer one walks with God, the greater will be the awareness of his sin. I recall as a child being fascinated by dust particles dancing about in a ray of sunlight beaming through my window. The dust was everywhere present, but was only made visible by the sunlight. So it is with sin. It is made manifest by the light of God's Word and Spirit. The brighter the light, the more evident the sin.

This was brought home to me through a comment by Serano Dwight, grandson and biographer of the great Jonathan Edwards. Edwards is considered by many to be the last of the Puritans and one of the greatest minds ever to grace the continent of North America. Like most of the Puritans he emphasized the reality of sin, even in the life of the believer. I often found myself wondering, "Where was the victory in their lives? They seem morbidly introspective." I've since concluded that their awareness of sin, as acute as it was, did not exceed their awareness and appreciation for God's grace in forgiving sin and even enhanced their grasp of victory.

Edwards, who was known as much for his holy life as for his remarkable intellect, reported having a "vastly greater sense of my own wickedness and the badness of my heart than ever I had before my conversion." In his opinion, this was a sign of spiritual health![12]

Feeling a need to clarify this apparent anomaly, Dwight explained that it wasn't that his grandfather *had* more wickedness, but that he had a greater *sense* of wickedness.

He then set out the following analogy:

> Suppose a blind man had a garden full of ugly and poisonous weeds. They are present in his garden but he is not aware of them. Now suppose that garden is, for the most part, cleared of the weeds, and many beautiful and worthwhile plants and flowers have replaced them. The man then regains his sight. There are fewer weeds, but he is more aware of them. So, the clearer our spiritual vision, the greater our awareness of sin.[13]

The words of J.C. Ryle, Anglican bishop of Liverpool, who died in the year 1900 eloquently summarize a balanced view of the subject:

> Sin—this infection of nature does remain, yes, even in them that are regenerate. So deeply planted are the roots of human corruption, that even after we are born again, renewed, washed, sanctified, justified and made living members of Christ, these roots remain alive in the bottom of our hearts and like the leprosy in the walls of the house, we never get rid of

---

[12] Jonathan Edwards, *The Works of Jonathan Edwards, Vol. I*, The Banner of Truth Trust, Carlisle, 1974, p. xlvii.
[13] Ibid.

them until the earthly house of this tabernacle is dissolved. Sin, no doubt, in the believer's heart, no longer has dominion. It is checked, controlled, mortified, and crucified by the expulsive power of the new principle of grace. The life of a believer is a life of victory and not of failure. But the very struggles that go on within him, the fight that he finds it needful to fight daily, the watchful jealousy he is obliged to exercise over his inner man, the contest between the flesh and the spirit, the inward groanings *which no one knows but he who has experienced them*—all testify to the same great truth: the enormous power and vitality of sin... Happy is the believer who understands it and, while he rejoices in Christ Jesus, has no confidence in the flesh, and while he says thanks be to God who gives us the victory, never forgets to watch and pray lest he fall into temptation.[14]

It is equally important to feel our abasement and to maintain it with a corresponding and proportionate exercise of faith. Let us lie low, but let us look high; let us realize our weakness and strength at the same moment.[15]

---

[14] J.C. Ryle, *Holiness*, op. cit., p. 5.
[15] Charles Bridges, The Christian Ministry, The Banner of Truth Trust, Edinburgh, 1830, 2001, p. 176.

Golf's Holy Grail—The Hole-in-One

"Have you ever had a hole-in-one?" Every serious golfer has been asked this question, probably more than once. It usually comes up after a near miss, a shot that had a chance of going in. Then the question is asked and the stories begin.

One of my favorites was from a guy I'd never met before. The occasion was more than a near miss, though. We were playing at Northwest Park when, on the hole just ahead of us, a shout of triumph went up. Yep, someone had just holed out on a par three from about 160 yards. Everyone within range entered into that golfer's joy.

Then my playing partner told me his story. He was on vacation in Orlando playing at one of the Disney World courses. They had a new and novel idea, where for a small fee, they video recorded you playing a hole. So, he paid the money and, wouldn't you know it, stroked a hole-in-one! I asked him if he looked at it often. He said whenever someone comes to his house, the very first thing they must do is sit down and watch it—it's mandatory viewing! I wonder if that includes the guy delivering pizza.

The next best thing to getting a hole-in-one is witnessing one. Carroll Valley Country Club in Fairfield, PA, finishes with a moderately difficult par three. For many years, several friends gathered for an annual golf vacation. I was playing in the last foursome with Larry. All the other groups were hanging around behind the green to watch us finish.

Larry was a fine golfer who was *not* having a fine day. It was so bad that he had lapsed into Larry Land. It's a place that serious golfers know well, only the name changes—a place of morbid, self-loathing that accompanies a lousy round. You know you've arrived there when you are thinking less about your next shot and more about what you're going to eat once the round is over.

It was my honor and I went to the tee, but then had second thoughts about club selection. "Go ahead, Larry," I said as I went back to change clubs. He then struck a perfect six iron with a slight draw that landed about fifteen feet short of the pin, checked up and rolled into the cup.

Larry's sixteen friends who formed a gallery around the green witnessed golf's *summum bonum*. At first, Larry didn't know what to do. He'd been grumping inwardly most of the day. It took a moment for what had just happened to sink in. Finally, he kicked into rejoicing mode. Oh, what a change a hole-in-one can bring to a golfer's day and the afterglow never entirely departs!

But as I stood there, happy for Larry, I suddenly realized that he'd taken my turn. Hey, wait a minute! Would that have been *my* hole-in-one? It's a theological question I've never been able to resolve.

My own hole-in-one story? Well, for many years I didn't really have one. Yeah, there was that time when I was sixteen, playing a practice round with some friends from my high school team at Montgomery Golf Club. We played our shots. It was early in the morning when no one else was around, so we decided to hit another shot on the same hole—and mine went in. It was an ugly shot. I toed a four iron, it landed short of the green, rolled up and into the hole. Still, I've kept the ball all these years, a hacked up Kro-Flite. That was my story. If I happened to mention it, someone was always sure to inform me, "You know, that was *not* a true hole-in-one." Okay, thanks for letting me know.

But then after fifty-five years of playing golf, it happened—the 170 yard fourth hole at Hampshire Green. On a day like any other day, May 31, 2016, I hit a five hybrid. It carried the trap, landing on the front of the green and, like it had eyes, rolled into the cup. For a moment it was hard to comprehend. I recall the kindness of my playing partners who were genuinely thrilled for me.

And then— I felt the favor of God. That's noteworthy because for the most part golf just punishes me. If the self-flagellants of the Middle Ages lived today, they wouldn't have to beat themselves with whips in holy procession. They would just play golf. It's much more painful. But at that moment I felt the opposite. As if I had come into the golfing equivalent of a state-of-grace. "O Lord, let now thy servant depart in peace, for I have had a hole-in-one!"

2: *Grace* and Justification

The Question Lurking in Every Heart

I can't remember much about the conversation. Her question seemed to come out of the blue. With a troubled look my cousin asked me, *"Why do I feel so guilty?"* It was the bluntness that caught me off guard. That was a long time ago. I can't even recall how I responded.

Guilt is out of favor these days. If you say to anyone, "I feel guilty," chances are they'll tell you that you shouldn't feel that way and then try to provide reasons why. Still, the question persists. It's a universal question. If she asked me today I would answer, "It's because you *are* guilty. And so am I. We all are."

Whether we feel guilty or not, we are. It is the human condition resulting from our sin against a holy God. I realize not everybody buys this. But it's true. It is what the Bible teaches. There is a God who is holy and just. He is completely opposed to sin. But he is also love. How a holy and just God can forgive guilty sinners is the love story of the cross. We've already touched on it a bit.

The catchall doctrine that summarizes this is called *justification*. Justification is that work of God that deals with our guilt problem. Many years ago, realizing the importance of this teaching, I made a determined effort to understand it. That proved to be one of the most valuable things I have ever done. Because for me personally, more than anything else, justification has helped me understand my relationship with God. As a pastor, on occasions too numerous to mention it has helped me help others. And in an even larger view, justification is the doctrine that protects the gospel. What could be more important than that?

Are We Okay?

Recently my wife asked me, "Are we okay?" She'd picked up something in my attitude that prompted the question. It led to a discussion. "Yeah, we're fine," I said, and then went on to explain what had been bothering me. She asked (and I've often asked the same of her) because being in right relationship as a married couple is fundamental to our well-being as individuals. My marriage to Clara is my primary human relationship. When we're not okay, everything else is affected.

What about your relationship with God? "Am I okay with God?" In some form we've probably all asked this or at least wondered about it. What would you say? I think most would reply, "I hope so." And to the logical follow-up, "How do I become okay?" we'd answer, "Just try to do my best and hope for the best."

How *does* a person become okay with God? How does a person become right with God? Or to use the more precise biblical-theological language, "How may a person be *justified* before God?" This is the fundamental question that we all must deal with.

The Apostle Paul wrote to Christians in Galatia around 45 AD:

> We know that a person is not justified by works of the law but through faith in Jesus Christ, so we also have believed in Christ Jesus, in order to be justified by faith in Christ and not by works of the law, because by works of the law no one will be justified.[1]

Here Paul contrasts two things—the works of the law[2] on one hand and faith in Christ on the other. In this one verse of Scripture Paul says the same thing no less than three times! How is a person justified before God? A person is justified *not* by works of the law, but through faith in Jesus Christ—faith in the simple gospel message that Jesus lived, died and rose.

Works of the law could refer to anything that a man might do with the intention of making himself acceptable to God. Things such as Sabbath-keeping, doing good deeds for the poor, etc. Things perhaps good in themselves but done with the motive of earning God's favor fall into this category *works of the law.* But Paul emphatically rejects this. The idea that a person can be justified, that is, make himself acceptable to God by doing works of the law, undercuts the gospel of grace.

Acceptance with God *does* rest on works, true. But whose work? The Christian gospel of grace insists that our

---

[1] Galatians 2.16.

[2] The phrase *works of the law* in the context of Galatians refers to the idea that Gentile Christians needed to be circumcised in order to become right with God; circumcision had been a requirement for Jews under the Old Covenant. Paul rejects the necessity of circumcision for Gentile believers.

acceptance rests on the work of the Son of God alone. We are justified by grace through what *Christ* has done. "... for all have sinned and fall short of the glory of God, and are justified by his grace as a gift, through the redemption that is in Christ Jesus...."[3]

Paul's insistence on grace is the main theme of his letter to the Galatians. Over the centuries, this foundational truth became obscured and the upside-down idea that man earns God's grace by his works gradually took hold. By the late Middle Ages the light of the gospel of grace had been eclipsed by the idea that a man could merit God's favor. The benefits of the gospel could no longer be felt.

Turning Point

The year 2017 marked the 500th anniversary of the Protestant Reformation. There is a famous statement associated with the Reformation that touches our theme:

*Justification is by grace alone,
through faith alone, in Christ alone.*

We need some background to understand the significance of this great statement. In Europe, a variety of unbiblical practices in the Roman Catholic Church had developed which veiled the gospel of grace. One practice in particular touched off a chain of events that sparked the Reformation. That practice was the sale of indulgences.

---

[3] Romans 3.23-24.

The church taught that when a person died, his soul did not go directly to heaven. No, it went to a place called Purgatory where the person was purged or purified from his remaining sins. In an ultimate sense it was granted that Christ died to save from guilt. But depending on how much you had sinned, you had to spend more or less time in Purgatory to be purified before you could enter heaven. According to many church authorities, Purgatory had purifying fires, purgatorial flames. It was a place of torment and it could go on for a long time.

But there was a way to lessen the time and pains of Purgatory—*indulgences*. An indulgence is a way to reduce the amount of punishment the soul endures in Purgatory. Indulgences consisted mainly of prayers and other religious works. But at some point, they came to be sold. It is easy to see how such a system would invite abuse.

A Dominican friar, Johann Tetzel, received special approval from the pope to sell indulgences in Germany.[4] He traveled around preaching emotional messages to the German peasantry imploring them to buy indulgences in order to relieve the torment of their relatives who were at that moment suffering in the flames. I've never heard any defense for Tetzel or his practices. He was the consummate religious huckster. He even had a jingle:

As soon as the coin in the coffer rings,
the soul from Purgatory springs.

A young Augustinian monk and university professor was outraged by this crass religious profiteering and felt he

---

[4] Funds raised by Tetzel were used to finance the construction of St. Peter's Basilica in Rome.

must do something. So, on October 31, 1517, Martin Luther walked up to the door of the Cathedral Church at Wittenburg and posted ninety-five theses opposing the abuse of indulgences. These were points for academic discussion. Nailing them to the door of the church was like posting them on the faculty bulletin board.

Luther was not an activist trying to start a fight. He was an academic trying to start a debate. He posted his theses in Latin. But others wrote them down and translated them into German. Then they quickly spread across Germany and beyond. This turned out to be the match that lit the fire we call the Protestant Reformation.

Luther and Justification by Grace Alone

What is it that Luther discovered? What is the essence of Protestantism? Of Christianity? What is it that makes Christianity different from every other religion on the face of the Earth? What is it that Luther discovered and of course, that Christ and the apostles brought to light through the gospel? That righteousness is not man's gift to God, it is God's gift to man.[5]

Protestantism was born out of the struggle for the doctrine of justification by faith alone. For Martin Luther, this was not simply one doctrine among others, but the "summary of all Christian doctrine," the article by which the church stands or falls.[6]

---

[5] D. James Kennedy, "By Faith Alone," taped message, n.d.
[6] Timothy George, *Theology of the Reformers*, Broadman Press, Nashville, 1988, p. 62.

Justification is the teaching that answers the question, "How does a man become right with God," or more specifically, "How does a sinful man become right with a holy God?"

> At the heart of the Christian faith lies the idea that human beings, finite and frail though they be, can enter into a relationship with the living God.[7]

From Scripture and throughout the course of the church's history, different images have been employed to express man's place in this relationship: as a slave needing redemption; a captive requiring ransom; a dead man in need of regeneration and resurrection, etc. In Luther's time the most common image was man as a guilty sinner in need of justification.[8]

Though he was short of stature, Martin Luther stands as a giant on the stage of world history. He was born into a German peasant family in 1483. His father, Hans, was a miner who became a mine-owner and eventually a man of some standing in his town.[9] Martin was usually cheerful and uncommonly intelligent. He worked hard, played the lute and had little trouble progressing in his studies, earning BA and MA degrees by the time he was 22. He was well on his way to becoming what his father hoped he would be—a lawyer. But Martin Luther was often troubled about the state of his soul and unsure of his relationship with God.

---

[7] Alister McGrath, *Christian Theology*, Blackwell Publishers, Oxford, 1994, 1997, p. 437.
[8] Ibid.
[9] John Legg, *The Footsteps of God*, The Evangelical Press, Welwyn, Hertfordshire, England, 1986, p. 78.

Luther's inner turmoil can be seen in three significant occurrences which shaped his life and his theological convictions.

Brush with Death

While he was in the middle of his masters' examinations, a close friend suddenly died. Shortly afterward as he was on his way back to the university, the sky darkened and a storm struck. A bolt of lightning either hit him or came so close that it knocked him to the ground. He was terrified and vowed on the spot to devote himself totally to the religious life by joining a monastery.

Luther's hasty vow was consistent with the fearful and superstitious temper of the times. Though the printing press was newly invented, it was still a medieval world. The modern era had not yet begun. A Renaissance had been going on in Italy, but Germany was still a cultural backwater. Luther lived in a world *lit only by fire*.[10] It was a world dominated by the church. But it was a corrupt church that used the fear of judgment to hold ignorant peasants in check.

Hans Luther was not pleased by his son's decision to enter a monastery. He had invested much in Martin's education. His parents expected him to prosper as a lawyer and care for them in their old age. But, though Martin loved his father, his concern for his own soul was greater. And in those times the best way to be sure of salvation was to dedicate oneself to religious life as a monk. So, within two weeks of his brush with death, Luther fulfilled his vow and

---

[10] To borrow Manchester's phrase.

entered the Augustinian monastery at Erfurt. It was July 1505 and he entered as a novice.

Among Luther's many fascinating traits two stand out: he was uncommonly aware and he was uncommonly conscientious. He was aware of the brevity of life, the holiness of God and of his own sinfulness. Luther was also absolutely conscientious in his new monastic life. But, "Here, in spite of fasting, scourging, the minutest self-examination and every form of self-discipline known to the strict order he had joined, he failed to find peace."[11]

By 1506, Luther had taken the vows of poverty, chastity and obedience and the following year, he was ordained as a priest. It was as he attempted to perform his first mass that a second significant event occurred.

First Mass

First mass for a new priest is a major event. Friends, family and relatives come from miles around. Hans Luther had come to terms with Martin's choice and had even made a contribution to the monastery. But in the middle of the mass Luther became overwhelmed by the majestic holiness of God and was unable to finish. In the language of the sixties, Luther freaked out. Another priest had to step in and complete the ceremony. His father was embarrassed and outraged. So, this is what it had come to. His brilliant son could not perform even the most common priestly duty.

The day was a disaster for Luther, but it pointed to what was to be his recurring problem for many years. He

---

[11] J.I. Packer, *The Bondage of the Will*, Revell, Westwood, 1957, p. 20.

used the word *anfectungen* to describe it. There is no one good English word to translate this. It refers to a feeling of dread, despair, anxiety—a sense of foreboding doom.

Luther was so aware of his own sin that he was constantly tormented by the question of whether he had fasted enough and prayed enough and done enough religious works to be accepted by God. He had totally submitted himself to the sacramental system of the Roman Catholic Church. But it provided him no relief, no peace. He wrote in later years,

> I was a good monk, and I kept the rule of my order so strictly that I may say that if ever a monk got to heaven by his monkery, it was I. All my brothers in the monastery who knew me will bear me out. If I had kept on any longer, I should have killed myself with vigils, prayers, reading and other work.[12]

One of the means the Church provided to comfort guilty consciences was the sacrament of penance, the confession of one's sins to a priest.

> Luther endeavored unremittingly to avail himself of this signal mercy. Without confession, he testified, the Devil would have devoured him long ago. He confessed frequently, often daily, and for as long as six hours on a single occasion. Every sin in order to be absolved was to be confessed. Therefore the soul must be searched and the memory ransacked and the motives probed. As an aid the penitent ran through the seven deadly sins and the Ten Commandments. Luther would repeat a confession and, to be sure of

---

[12] Roland Bainton, *Here I Stand*, Abingdon Press, Nashville, 1950, p. 45.

including everything, would review his entire life until the confessor grew weary and exclaimed, "Man, God is not angry with you. You are angry with God. Don't you know God commands you to hope?"

This assiduous confessing certainly succeeded in clearing up any major transgressions. The leftovers with which Luther kept trotting in appeared to his confessor to be only the scruples of a sick soul. "Look here," said he, "if you expect Christ to forgive you, come in with something to forgive—murder, blasphemy, adultery—instead of all these peccadilloes."[13]

But something was accomplished through all this. Luther became aware that there was something much deeper that was the matter. Something more than "... any particular list of offenses which could be enumerated, confessed and forgiven. The very nature of man is corrupt...."[14] The entire man is in need of forgiveness.

Preaching the Bible

Aware of his sin and conscientious to a fault, Luther soldiered on in this state of turmoil for some years. Then, in 1511, his mentor and superior at the monastery, Johann Von Staupitz, stunned him by suggesting that he should prepare himself for the ministry of preaching. Luther was amazed at the suggestion, feeling himself entirely unfit for such an endeavor. But Staupitz prevailed and the move proved to be of great significance, for it meant Luther would have to study the Bible.

---

[13] Ibid, p. 54.
[14] Ibid, p. 55.

He hardly knew anything about the Bible, not even having seen one until he was twenty years old. He studied with characteristic diligence and received the degree of Doctor of Theology. In 1513 he began preaching from Psalms, followed by Romans in 1515 and Galatians in 1517. The result of all this study of Scripture brought Luther face to face with the God whose judgment he dreaded. But a great climax of spiritual discovery was at hand. As he himself described it years later:

> I greatly longed to understand Paul's Epistle to the Romans and nothing stood in the way but that one expression, "the justice of God," because I took it to mean that justice whereby God is just and deals justly in punishing the unjust. My situation was that, although an impeccable monk, I stood before God as a sinner troubled in conscience, and I had no confidence that my merit would assuage him. Therefore I did not love a just and angry God, but rather hated and murmured against him. Yet I clung to the dear Paul and had a great yearning to know what he meant.
>
> Night and day I pondered until I saw the connection between the justice of God and the statement that "the just shall live by his faith." Then I grasped that the justice of God is that righteousness by which through grace and sheer mercy God justifies us through faith. Thereupon I felt myself to be reborn and to have gone through open doors into paradise. The whole of Scriptures took on a new meaning, and whereas before the "justice of God" had filled me with hate, now it became to me inexpressibly sweet

in greater love. This passage of Paul became to me a gate to heaven....[15]

This doctrine—justification by grace alone, through faith alone, in Christ alone—that meant so much to Luther personally was to become the very foundation of the Protestant Reformation. Justification was the answer to Luther's concerns about the state of his soul. It brought about reconciliation and peace with the God whom he greatly feared. What he had tried to earn by religious works he finally realized was a gift from God to be received through simple trust.

> Therefore no one will be declared righteous in his sight by observing the law; rather, through the law we become conscious of sin. But now a righteousness from God, apart from law, has been made known, to which the Law and the Prophets testify. This righteousness from God comes through faith in Jesus Christ to all who believe. There is no difference, for all have sinned and fall short of the glory of God, and are justified freely by his grace through the redemption that came by Christ Jesus.[16]

Justification is that act of God by which He pardons (forgives) all our sins and accepts us as righteous in his sight. This is possible because of what Jesus Christ has done in dying on the cross for our sins. Justification is all of grace, meaning God didn't have to do it, being under no obligation. And it is all of faith, meaning it must be received as a gift. It cannot be earned.

---

[15] Ibid, p. 65.
[16] Romans 3.20-24 (NIV).

The language of justification comes from the law court. In justification God the Judge pronounces or declares a person righteous. Such a declaration does not *make* a person righteous in the sense that character transformation has occurred. But the justified person's status has changed from that of a condemned sinner to one no longer under condemnation.

Imagine yourself standing before the bar in God's courtroom. You know you are guilty and deserving of punishment. But Another has graciously stepped in to take your place and receive your punishment. So, God acquits you! The acquittal is full and final. Your status has changed from guilty to righteous.

God has shown amazing grace in sending His Son to die for us. How great is the love of the Son of God, that he would take our place, suffer excruciating pain and separation from his Father to pay the price of our redemption. It's even more amazing when we consider that he did this for us when we were his enemies![17]

It is important to remember that through justification, though our legal status has changed, our character has not. Justification is a legal declaration of righteousness. It is the opposite of a pronouncement of condemnation. It cancels our legal liability before God (Romans 8.1) and confers upon us a privileged status (Romans 8.33), giving us all the rights of those who had never sinned. Justification saves from the past and secures for the future (Romans

---

[17] Romans 5.10.

8.34-39); it is an irreversible pronouncement (Romans 8.30,33).[18]

> God's justifying decision is in effect the judgment of the Last Day regarding where we will spend eternity, brought forward into the present and pronounced here and now. It is a judgment on our eternal destiny; God will never go back on it, however much Satan may appeal against the verdict.[19]

For Luther, it was never enough to merely know *that* Christ died or *why* Christ died.

> It was that Christ died *for me*! Read with great emphasis these words, **me, *for me***, and accustom yourself to accept and apply to yourself this ***me*** with certain faith.[20]

The idea of a gracious justification coming to us as a gift is so foreign to us that Luther said of this teaching, "We must beat it into their heads!" The greater the awareness of our plight, the greater will be the appreciation of our justification. Luther knew his sin, but he also knew his Justifier, the One who died for him. The knowledge of this great truth opened for him the gates of heaven and changed the course of the world's history.[21]

---

[18] Character transformation occurs under a different but related work called *sanctification*, which we will look at in the next section.
[19] *Geneva Study Bible*, Thomas Nelson Publishers, Nashville, 1995, p.1852.
[20] Timothy George, *Theology of the Reformers*, The Broadman Press, Nashville, 1988, p. 60.
[21] It was also significant in the English and American Great Awakening two centuries later.

Luther's life demonstrates the beneficial effect of justification on a personal level, providing the proper orientation of life in relation to God. But on another level *justification also serves to protect the gospel.* We are so inclined to justify ourselves by the things that we do—how religious we are, how much we pray or read the Bible or help the poor or whatever may be our inclination. There is nothing wrong with these things in themselves. We ought to do them. But never as the ground for our acceptance with God.

By the works of the law no one will be justified! The danger is that we try to smuggle our good works in through the back door and then say to God, "Look at all that I have done. Accept me on this basis." To which he would reply, "Why? Was the sacrifice of my Son insufficient?"

> ... for all have sinned and fall short of the glory of God, and are justified by his grace as a gift, through the redemption that is in Christ Jesus....[22]

Justification is free, a gift of grace that can never be earned. It can only be received as a gift. Faith is but the hand reaching out to receive it. I love the doctrine of justification because it protects the gospel. I love the gospel because I love Jesus. And I love Jesus because he *first* loved me.

---

[22] Romans 3.23-24.

3: *Grace* and Sanctification

Sanctification, says the Westminster Shorter Catechism (Q. 35), is "the work of God's free grace, whereby we are renewed in the whole man after the image of God, and are enabled more and more to die unto sin, and live unto righteousness." The concept is not of sin being totally eradicated (that is to claim too much) or merely counteracted (that is to say too little), but of a divinely wrought character change freeing us from sinful habits and forming in us Christlike affections, dispositions, and virtues.[1]

Running the Race Set Before Us

In my junior year of high school, we were required to be timed in a long-distance run. While not an outstanding athlete, I could hold my own in most sports. Distance running was different. It was hard. Not complicated, just hard and painful and I wasn't into pain. During the regular gym class cross-country unit, some friends and I contrived a shortened course that took us through the school building, down the hall where the typing classes were held and out again onto the field. In this way, we knocked about a quarter mile off the course—until the typing teacher got wise to the thundering hoof beats outside her classroom.

The time came to be timed. Normally I would have turned in a marginal performance, but for some forgotten reason, I decided to give it my all. Summoning some

---

[1] J.I. Packer, *Concise Theology*, Tyndale House, Wheaton, 1993, p. 169.

previously unknown inner fortitude I pushed myself beyond measure and turned in a remarkable performance. It was so good that the cross-country coach heard about it and tried to recruit me for the school team. I gave him the same answer I gave my mom when she suggested I take ballet lessons with my sisters: "No thanks."

"But Robin," she said, "boys do ballet." Not this boy.

I felt like I was going to die after that race, and no wonder. I'd done nothing to train for it so I wasn't in shape to persevere. Over the years I've gained respect for distance runners. It is a great analogy for understanding the Christian life, as this passage from Hebrews shows:

> Therefore, since we are surrounded by so great a cloud of witnesses, let us also lay aside every weight, and sin which clings so closely, and let us run with endurance the race that is set before us, looking to Jesus, the founder and perfecter of our faith, who for the joy that was set before him endured the cross, despising the shame, and is seated at the right hand of the throne of God.[2]

A great cloud of witnesses, heroic men and women of biblical history—Abraham, Moses, Sarah—ran their races faithfully as examples to us all (Hebrews 11). There are other helpful analogies in Scripture for understanding the Christian life, but the distance race motif provides much food for thought. This kind of race requires perseverance, discipline and training. And though it is not particularly complicated (you put one foot in front of the other, over and over again) great distance runners have been among our more intelligent athletes. They are able to marshal their

---

[2] Hebrews 12.1-2.

resources for the long haul, focusing on the task at hand, one step at a time.

The Christian life is a marathon, no matter when you begin. It is not a sprint. There is a course marked out by God for each of us. Your course is specifically tailored by God for his glory and your good. There is no short course to Christian maturity, no crossless way to follow Christ, no instant secret to the Christian life, no shortcut past the typing classrooms.

Yet, for those who are called to follow in the pathway of discipleship, God makes his ways known and grants the power and presence of his Spirit to guide us as he transforms us. The theological category for this is *sanctification*. Beginning at a definite point in time, it refers to that process by which we become more and more like our Lord Jesus Christ.[3]

> Jesus said to his disciples: *You therefore must be perfect as your heavenly Father is perfect.*[1]

I had just finished a sermon that touched on the topic of anger so I invited any who wanted prayer to come forward. About twenty humble saints responded, a significant percentage of our small Lancaster, PA church plant. But it wasn't the number that surprised me. It was that nineteen of the twenty were young mothers and I knew most of them.

I knew what they were experiencing. I knew because I was married to a young mother facing the same constant demands, like not even being able to go to the bathroom

---

[3] Romans 8.29.

without little hands appearing under the door. I knew that they were conscientious Christians. And I knew what led them to respond was their frustration at being caught in the gap between the biblical standard of self-control and their own failed efforts to live up to that standard.

Whether it's anger, fear, lust, jealousy or something as common as discouragement, we've all experienced the gap between what we are and what we know we should be. The Bible calls us victors, new creations, overcomers, not just conquerors—but *more* than conquerors.[4] Some days we may even feel that way. But more often than not, we have a hard time reconciling our daily experience with the victorious Christian life we hear about.

There seems to be this gap between God's expectation of us and what we are actually achieving; between what we ought to be and what we are; between what we know and how we live. If the gap becomes great enough, we're seen as hypocrites. And if it gets even bigger, the police might be called!

This gap is a fact of Christian life. Most of us don't need anyone to point out our lack of consistency. Though we might minimize it, we're all too aware of it. Such awareness is meant to keep us humble and dependent on God. But if we are ignorant of the Bible's teaching on sanctification we can be trapped into thinking we are simply losers, failures, maybe not even Christians at all. Worse yet, it can make us doubt the truth of God's Word and God's faithfulness. After all, it is written, "He who began a good work in you will bring it to completion at the day of Jesus Christ."[5]

---

[4] Romans 8.37.
[5] Philippians 1.6.

How are we to understand the apparent contradiction between what God reckons us to be and what we, by experience, know ourselves to be? Paul assured the Corinthians, "You were washed, you were sanctified, you were justified in the name of the Lord Jesus Christ and by the Spirit of our God."[6] Sounds pretty clear. But we know from the larger context of the letter that there were serious moral problems in Corinth, from incest to drunkenness. And in a follow up letter he writes: "Let us purify ourselves from everything that contaminates body and spirit, perfecting holiness out of reverence for God."[7] I suspect the Corinthians may have been confused. Were they sanctified or contaminated? Actually they were both, and so are we. To explain this, we need to go on a brief tangent.

God's kingdom, of which we are citizens, is both "now" and "not yet." In certain respects, it is present. In other respects, it is future. Jesus came proclaiming and demonstrating that the kingdom (the reign) of God had broken into human history. He said, "If I drive out demons by the finger of God, then the kingdom of God has come to you."[8]

However, that kingdom has not come in its fullness. That won't occur until Jesus returns in power, when every knee shall bow and every tongue confess that he is Lord. Until then, without denying the present reality of God's kingdom, we pray, "May your kingdom *come*."[9] In other words, the kingdom of God is both present *and* future.

---

[6] I Corinthians 6.11.
[7] II Corinthians 7.1.
[8] Luke 11.20.
[9] Matthew 6.10.

In this way God's kingdom parallels our individual lives. God has declared us righteous—now. Our legal standing before him has changed from condemned to justified. That issue has been forever settled in the high court of heaven. But our spiritual growth is an ongoing project—a work in progress.

So, do we have victory in Jesus or not? Are we overcomers or are we overcome? Oscar Cullmann suggested a helpful analogy from WW II that can shed some light on this paradox.[10]

History records two important days toward the end of the war, D-Day and VE Day. D-Day took place June 6, 1944 when Allied forces landed on the beaches of Normandy. This was the turning point of the war. The success of this landing sealed Hitler's fate. But though the war was essentially won, total victory in Europe (VE Day) did not occur till May 7, 1945 when the Germans surrendered in Berlin. This eleven-month interval was one of the bloodiest periods of the war as pitched battles were fought throughout France, Belgium and Germany.

The cross was our D-Day. There the Lord Jesus Christ died to break the chains of sin that bound his people. On the basis of his death and resurrection we are justified. Yet the final victory awaits Christ's return. The outcome is not in doubt. Yet we still find ourselves involved in skirmishes and battles that are sometimes severe. This will be the case until the Lord appears in glory to utterly vanquish the powers of darkness.

---

[10] Oscar Cullmann, *Christ and Time*, Westminster Press, Philadelphia, 1964, p. 3.

If we keep this distinction in mind it can spare us needless discouragement. The battle still rages but the war has been won. An awareness of Christ's finished work on our behalf is essential as we pursue sanctification in union with Him.

How does a person change? How does a person grow, become more like Christ? The doctrine of sanctification answers these questions. Various branches of the church have handled this somewhat differently, of course. But there are areas of general agreement.

The meaning of the word *sanctify* is "to set apart; to consecrate." (*Holiness* comes from the same Greek root.) It may pertain to a person, place, occasion or object. When something is sanctified, it is separated from common use and devoted to special use. For example, the Day of Atonement was set apart (sanctified) to the holy God, making it a holy day. A thing sanctified is not made holy simply by being set apart; it derives its holiness from the One to whom it is devoted. Because only God is holy, he alone can impart holiness.

The term *sanctification* primarily describes the process believers undergo as the Spirit of God works in us to make us like Christ. That process begins the moment we are regenerated and continues as long as we live. It is marked by daily conflict as we appropriate the grace and strength of God to overcome indwelling sin. The *guilt* of sin has already been removed through the justifying work of God. Sanctification removes the *pollution* of sin:

> By *guilt* we mean the state of deserving condemnation or of being liable to punishment because God's law has been violated. In justification, which is a declarative act of God, the guilt of our sin is removed

on the basis of the atoning work of Jesus Christ. By *pollution*, however, we mean the corruption of our nature which is the result of sin and which, in turn, produces further sin. As a result of the Fall of our first parents, we are all born in a state of corruption; the sins which we commit are not only products of that corruption but also add to it. In *sanctification*, the pollution of sin is in the process of being removed (though it will not be totally removed until the life to come).[11]

The Bible presents sanctification as *growth in godliness*. This is devotion to God and the character that springs from devotion. Such qualities as love for God, desire for God and a proper fear of God form the soul of godliness. Another word that expresses this is *piety*, an older term that sadly has fallen out of use. It combines the ideas of loving God and fearing him.

Godliness involves more than morality or zeal. It springs from a union with Christ and a passion to honor him. A godly person wishes to be like her Lord and to please him. She wants to feel what God feels, to think his thoughts after him, to do his will. She wants to take upon herself the character of God so that he might be glorified. No endeavor is more worthy of our life-long effort: "For physical training is of some value, but godliness has value for all things, holding promise for both the present life and the life to come."[12]

Unlike justification, which is entirely a work of God on our behalf, sanctification is a joint effort of grace requiring

---

[11] Anthony A. Hoekema, *Saved By Grace*, Eerdmans Publishing Co., Grand Rapids, 1989, pp. 192-93.
[12] I Timothy 4.8.

our cooperation. *We* are called to work out our salvation with fear and trembling, for *God works in us*, to accomplish his good pleasure.[13] But even though we are a necessary part of this operation, it is no less a work of grace. The very desire and ability we contribute comes from God himself. Besides, God's grace is not opposed to our effort, just to the idea of earning.

> For the grace of God has appeared, bringing salvation for all people, training us to renounce ungodliness and worldly passions and to live self-controlled, upright and godly lives in the present age, waiting for our blessed hope, the appearing of the glory of our great God and Savior Jesus Christ, who gave himself for us, to redeem us from all lawlessness and to purify for himself a people for his own possession who are zealous for good works.[14]

The New Testament charts a course for holy living which is a middle way (actually a higher way) between legalism on one side and license on the other. Church traditions that place the accent too heavily on God's work within us without expecting that work to result in a growing desire for godliness can veer off the path toward license.

> For, as I have often told you before and now say again even with tears, many live as enemies of the cross of Christ. Their destiny is destruction, their god is their stomach, and their glory is in their shame. Their mind is on earthly things.[15]

---

[13] Philippians 2.12-13.
[14] Titus 2.11-14.
[15] Philippians 3.18-19 (NIV).

On the other hand, there are those who have so emphasized man's part that they elevate technique over truth and end in legalism. Of course, there are varying degrees of these driftings.

The Finish Line

What is the goal in all this? When Paul writes, "Let us therefore, *as many as are perfect*, have this attitude; and if in anything you have a different attitude, God will reveal that also to you," (Philippians 3.15, NAS) what does he mean? When Jesus exhorts, "*Be ye perfect*, therefore, as your heavenly Father is perfect," (Matthew 5.48, KJV) what does he have in mind? Do they really expect us to attain perfection?

Yearning for perfection has inspired many to pursue God. Throughout human history poets and philosophers have longed to regain a lost innocence and perfection. Scripture directs us to be perfect but it also shows that sinless perfection is out of our reach in this life. This presents us with a dilemma. We may not throw up our hands in defeat, but neither may we adopt an unrealistic "can do" attitude toward perfection that's more in line with positive thinking than with the Bible.

The way forward comes when we see that the Bible presents perfection in two ways. Paul's vision for the Philippians was maturity. The New International Version translates Paul's comment, "All of us who are *mature* should take such a view of things."[16] The "perfect" in this

---

[16] Philippians 3.15 (NIV, emphasis added).

sense may best be described as "those who have made reasonable progress in spiritual growth and stability."[17]

It is really a question of making progress in grace and godliness—a matter of growth. It's natural for every child to want to grow. This is no less true for the believer. So, rather than taking a casual or haphazard approach to growth, we must let the call to perfection urge us onward in a serious quest to be more like Jesus. Paul's own example is the model:

> Not that I have already obtained this or am already perfect, but I press on to make it my own, because Christ Jesus has made me his own. Brothers, I do not consider that I have made it my own. But one thing I do: forgetting what lies behind and straining forward to what lies ahead, I press on toward the goal for the prize of the upward call of God in Christ Jesus.[18]

A second use of *perfect* may be seen in Paul's first letter to the Corinthians, "When the perfect comes, the partial will pass away."[19] Here, *perfect* is restricted to the Godhead—perfection that awaits the return of Christ. But John writes:

> Beloved, we are God's children now, and what we will be has not yet appeared; but we know that when he appears we shall be like him, because we shall see

---

[17] Richard B. Gaffin (study notes from NIV Study Bible, Zondervan, Grand Rapids, 1985, p. 2290.)
[18] Philippians 3.12-14.
[19] I Corinthians 13.10.

him as he is. And everyone who thus hopes in him purifies himself even as he is pure.[20]

John's words indicate that we who trust in Christ and hope in him are at this moment being purified *and* at his appearance will actually be like him!

The Westminster Shorter Catechism makes this explicit when it asks "What benefits do believers receive from Christ at death?" and answers, "The souls of believers are at their death made perfect in holiness…."[21] From the moment we become Christians we are "enrolled in heaven."[22] Those thus enrolled will be among the spirits of the righteous made perfect at their death.[23] And when our Lord Jesus Christ returns, our bodies will be glorified, our redemption made complete, and best of all we will always be with the Lord![24]

---

[20] I John 3.2-3.
[21] Westminster Shorter Catechism, Question 37.
[22] Chad Van Dixhoorn, *Confessing the Faith*, Banner of Truth Trust, Carlisle, 2014, p. 428.
[23] Hebrews 12.23.
[24] Romans 8.18-23; I Corinthians 15.50-53; I Thessalonians 4.16-17.

4: *Grace* and Change

How does this change occur? What provision has God made for our progress in grace? How do we overcome sin and live victorious lives in Christ? The sixth chapter of Paul's letter to the Roman Christians has long been recognized for its essential contribution to the doctrine of sanctification. In it we find Paul contending for a proper understanding of what it means to live as a Christian. But it would be a mistake to jump into Romans 6 without regard to its context, so a brief review of the letter to this point is in order.

Romans is more systematic than any of Paul's other letters in displaying his understanding of salvation. After some introductory remarks, he levels a stinging indictment of the entire human race, Jew and Gentile, showing that all men are guilty before God. Then he explains how God justifies sinners through faith in Jesus Christ. This is the gist of the first four chapters.

In the beginning of Chapter 5 Paul speaks of the benefits that come to us as a result of Christ's justifying work. We now have peace with God and rejoice in the hope of his glory. We can even rejoice in the trials and tribulations we encounter because God uses them to develop our character and produce hope in us. God's love has been poured out upon us through the Holy Spirit. Since all this was done for us when we were his enemies, we can be completely assured of continued grace now that we are his friends.

123

In the latter part of the chapter he sketches a comparison and contrast between Adam and Jesus Christ, the two representative heads of the human race. He shows that Christ's obedience[1] way more than compensates for the misery and condemnation caused by Adam's disobedience.[2] The chapter then ends with these words:

> Now the law came in to increase the trespass, but *where sin increased, grace abounded all the more*, so that, as sin reigned in death, grace also might reign through righteousness leading to eternal life through Jesus Christ our Lord.[3]

Paul would prefer to go on describing the blessings of justification, but he pauses, realizing that his words could be misinterpreted to imply that he is saying we should go on sinning so that grace might abound all the more. That is how Chapter 6 begins.

The gospel of grace, rightly preached will always be open to the charge that it promotes lawlessness. It's not a valid charge, but it was made in Paul's day and it continues to be made today. Paul's opponents accused him of teaching that since people were freely forgiven by grace, their conduct did not matter.

Their faulty reasoning was as follows: If God forgives us freely by grace (which he does) and if it is true that God's grace is magnified in forgiving sin (which it is), then why not

---

[1] Romans 5.19.
[2] Romans 5.17.
[3] Romans 5.20-21 (emphasis added).

sin all the more, so that more grace flows and God receives more glory.[4]

"Not so fast!" says Paul. "You're missing something fundamental. Through the gospel we *died* to sin. And since that is the case, how can we go on living in it?"[5] The rest of the chapter counters the charge of lawlessness (or antinomianism). While answering his critics, Paul supplies us with some of the Bible's richest teaching on sanctification and what it means to be in union with our Lord Jesus Christ.

Union with Christ

We can all look back on those who have influenced our lives: parents, a special friend, a coach or teacher. But Jesus Christ is different from all others. It is certainly true that many who are not Christians have been influenced by our Lord's example and teaching (Gandhi comes to mind). But the New Testament teaches genuine faith in Christ establishes a relationship infinitely more penetrating and significant than mere moral influence. Paul writes about us being "in Christ" and Christ being "in us." The implications of this mysterious union are without exaggeration, astounding. John R.W. Stott has written:

---

[4] The Russian charlatan, Rasputin, who posed as a holy man to gain access to the royal family, successfully seduced many women using this line: "Let us sin, my dear, if sin it is. God will receive glory in forgiving us." Cf. F.F. Bruce, *The Letter of Paul to the Romans: An Introduction and Commentary*, Eerdmans Publishing Co., Grand Rapids, 1963, p. 134.
[5] Romans 6.2.

The great theme of Romans 6, and in particular verses 1-11, is that the death and resurrection of Jesus Christ are not only historical facts and significant doctrines, but personal experiences of the Christian believer. They are events in which we ourselves have come to share. All Christians have been united to Christ in his death and resurrection. Further, if this is true, if we have died with Christ and risen with Christ, it is inconceivable that we should go on living in sin.[6]

The following passage from Romans 6 highlights this union with Christ:

Do you not know that all of us who have been baptized into Christ Jesus were baptized into his death? We were buried therefore *with* him by baptism into death, in order that, just as Christ was raised from the dead by the glory of the Father, we too might walk in newness of life. For if we have been united *with* him in a death like his, we shall certainly be united *with* him in a resurrection like his. We know that our old self was crucified *with* him in order that the body of sin might be brought to nothing, so that we would no longer be enslaved to sin.[7]

Here, Paul uses the act of baptism to remind us of these truths. What he is eager to show, however, is not baptism but the faith that leads to baptism. That faith effects a spiritual union with Jesus Christ.

---

[6] John R.W. Stott, *Men Made New*, Baker Book House, Grand Rapids, 1966, 1984, p. 30.
[7] Romans 6.3-6 (emphasis added).

Jesus actually conquered death. This is an awesome truth. Yet as amazing as this is, what is even more remarkable is that *we* are considered to be united with him in his death, burial and resurrection. That little preposition *with* has immense significance since it represents our association, our union with Jesus Christ in his death, burial and resurrection—in his gospel! In a related letter Paul writes,

> I have been crucified with Christ. It is no longer I who live, but Christ who lives in me. And the life I now live in the flesh I live by faith in the Son of God who loved me and gave himself for me.[8]

All Christians, not just a spiritual elite, are united to Christ. If one is not united to him he is not a Christian. This union is a living relationship that provides us with grace to overcome sin and live victorious lives. Jesus is the author and finisher of our faith. He is the captain of our salvation. He is the pioneer who has gone before us and on our behalf conquered sin and death. Sinclair Ferguson has described him as the lead climber of a team scaling a mountain. We're roped to him. And just as surely as he has triumphed, so will we.[9]

Jesus uses the picture of a vine and its branches to show this relationship. He tells us to abide in him, for apart from him, we can do nothing. This imagery also indicates that the relationship is living, not static. We are alive and

---

[8] Galatians 2.20.
[9] Sinclair Ferguson, *Christian Spirituality: Five Views of Sanctification*, D.L. Alexander, ed. InterVarsity Press, Downers Grove, 1988, p. 49.

growing in union with our Lord Jesus. This is true whether we feel it to be so or not.

The closest human analogy is the marriage relationship. Two people come together to form a new entity, a union where the two become one. They retain their individual identities, but they merge in a way unique, mysterious and wonderful. Though they may not always *feel* united, they *are* united. The woman takes the name of her husband demonstrating her submission to him. The husband assumes responsibility for his wife's support and protection. They hold all assets and liabilities in common and wear rings as symbolic evidence of their special relationship.

So it is when we are wed to Jesus Christ, our heavenly bridegroom. Though we retain our personalities, they are being transformed as we become partakers of the divine nature. We are no longer the same. As Christians, we have taken the name of Christ, identifying with him for better or for worse no matter the cost. We bring our assets and liabilities into the relationship and so does he. (What an apparently bad deal for Jesus—he gets our sin and we get his righteousness!) And in baptism, we receive the sign of the covenant, the ring that shows we belong to him.

This union is enduring. It is eternal. Jesus reassured his disciples with the promise, "Where I am, there you may be also."[10] One day in unbroken fellowship we will enjoy the fullness of his presence in glorified form. It is also a union of perfect acceptance. When the Father thinks of you, he never thinks of you apart from Christ. He always sees you as "in Christ." Therefore, how he thinks of Christ is how he thinks of you. Is he pleased with Jesus? He is just as pleased

---

[10] John 14.3.

with you, in Christ. Imagine the revolution in our lives if we would keep in mind the fact that we are united with Christ!

We Died to Sin

Going back to Romans 6.3, recall that Paul said "we died to sin." That small phrase is the key to understanding the chapter but it has been often misinterpreted, sometimes with catastrophic results.

One popular Bible teacher takes Paul to mean that sin no longer exerts any influence on the Christian. He poses the question: If you prop a dead man against the wall and then parade before him scantily-clad women, what effect would it have on him? No effect at all, because he's dead. Sin can no longer entice him.

But though appealing, this interpretation contradicts experience and renders unintelligible a multitude of biblical warnings to avoid sin. In Romans 6.12-14 Paul urges us not to yield our bodies to sin, an admonition entirely unnecessary if we are dead and unable to be enticed. Those who think themselves beyond temptation should consider Paul's warning to the Corinthians, "Therefore let anyone who thinks that he stands take heed lest he fall."[11]

Sometimes, along with this wrong interpretation is the view that Paul's phrase should be understood as an imperative, a command, something we must perform. Then the next step is to insist that the believer have 'a death to sin' or 'death to self' experience. But if we see 'dying to sin'

---

[11] I Corinthians 10.12.

as something we must perform, we're headed for discouragement.

Such thinking often produces a struggle to project an outward appearance of victory while on the inside the man is a mass of frustration. Then when such a person runs out of gas, he loses hope for trying again, thinking, "I gave it my best shot, maybe I'm just not cut out for Christianity."

But there is another way to understand the phrase "we died to sin." Ferguson has it right when he says, "Paul is not telling us to do something; he is analyzing something that has taken place."[12] Despite our ongoing vulnerability to temptation, two things can be said with certainty for those who believe and have been united with Christ:

1. **We died to the *penalty* (or guilt) of sin.** Scripture says "the wages of sin is death" (Romans 6.23). Death is the penalty for sin. Yet our Lord's death eliminated that penalty for us when he experienced death on the cross. Because we are 'in him' we died 'with him' to that penalty. "Therefore, there is now no condemnation to those who are in Christ Jesus."[13]

2. **We died to the *reign* of sin.** As a result of our union with Christ in his death, we are no longer obligated to sin. This means not that we are *not* able to sin, but that we are able *not* to sin. Paul reasons that since Christ died to sin and since we, in our union with him, also died to sin, sin no longer has dominion over us, just as it no longer has dominion

---

[12] Ferguson, op. cit., p. 55.
[13] Romans 8.1.

over him. "For sin shall not be your master, because you are not under law, but under grace."[14]

Slavery is a prominent theme in Romans 6, where two types of slavery are presented. Before becoming Christians, we were slaves to sin. We had no choice but to sin. But now that we are in Christ that has changed. The master-slave relationship with sin has been broken. Sin no longer dominates our lives. We are still slaves, but we are slaves to God. He is now our master. The wonderful paradox is that the one who is God's slave is free indeed!

Walking It Out

So much for the foundation for victory. How does it work out in actual practice? When counseling others, I have found it helpful to point out three markers from Romans 6 as ways to grow in grace.

1. **Know the truth!**

> "**We know** that our old self was crucified with him in order that the body of sin might be brought to nothing, so that we would no longer be enslaved to sin." (Romans 6.6)

We must first *know* this in order to believe it. Spiritual knowledge precedes faith. Memorizing Romans 6 has been a great help for me and many others. That's because memorizing leads to meditation and its associated benefits

---

[14] Romans 6.14.

(cf. Joshua 1.8). In Romans 8.6 (NIV) Paul says that "the mind controlled by the Spirit is life and peace." What better way to be spiritually-minded than to have your mind filled with Spirit-inspired truth? Knowing the truth is the prelude to the truth setting us free.

It is much easier to follow Jesus' example of fighting temptation with the Word of God[15] when that word has been stored in our hearts. "I have hidden your word in my heart that I might not sin against you."[16] As we memorize and meditate on scriptural truth we are transformed from spiritual pushovers who cave in to the slightest temptation into spiritual warriors who say, "I died to sin; how can I live in it any longer?"[17]

2. Consider it to be true!

> "For the death he died he died to sin once for all, but the life he lives he lives to God. So you also must **consider yourselves dead to sin** and alive to God in Christ Jesus."[18]

"This is no game of let's pretend," writes F.F. Bruce. "Believers should consider themselves to be what God in fact has made them."[19] Because we are in fact dead to sin, the penalty and guilt of sin are no longer factors for us. We have Jesus to thank for that. But beyond this, we are no longer obligated to sin, because sin is no longer our master. Its dominion has ended. And not only have we died to sin

---

[15] Matthew 4.1-11.
[16] Psalm 119.11 (NIV).
[17] Romans 6.2.
[18] Romans 6.10-11 (emphasis added).
[19] Bruce, op. cit., pp. 129-130.

but we are alive to God *in* Christ Jesus! This phrase brings us back once again to our blessed union with Christ and all the benefits associated with that happy state of affairs.

"Consider yourselves dead to sin" uses an accounting term which could be translated, "count" or "reckon" or "calculate." If I told you I had deposited money in your bank account and I was trustworthy, you would count on the money being there. In essence, Paul is saying, don't act like a pauper, because you are not one. You are a child of God with abundant resources. Consider it to be so!

3. Present yourselves to God!

> "Do not present your members to sin as instruments for unrighteousness, but **present yourselves to God** as those who have been brought from death to life, and your members to God as instruments for righteousness."[20]

We have choices to make—many choices—every day. We may offer the parts of our bodies (our members) to God for use in righteousness, or we may offer them for wicked use. Our minds, our tongues, eyes and other body parts are themselves morally neutral. But the way in which our hearts direct them determine whether we honor God or grieve him. Sinful habits do not develop overnight. Likewise, it is through persistent application of truth that they are replaced and overcome. This requires perseverance.

Jesus said, "What comes out of a person is what defiles him. For from within, out of the heart of man, come evil thoughts, sexual immorality, theft, murder, adultery,

---

[20] Romans 6.13 (emphasis added).

coveting, wickedness, deceit, sensuality, envy, slander, pride, foolishness. All these evil things come from within, and they defile a person."[21] Notice that what heads the list is "evil thoughts."

Evil actions begin as evil thoughts. Thus, it is in our thoughts first of all, that the battle must be won. The battle begins in our minds. Changing our ways of thinking will change our ways of acting. And our thinking will change as we meditate on biblical truth.

I knew a woman who was plagued by fearful and depressing thoughts stemming from sins committed against her in the past. Her thoughts kept her in a spiritual prison. When she reflected upon them, as she often did, or was faced with a current difficulty, the phonograph needle in her mind would come down and begin playing a familiar old blues LP.[22] Thought patterns over the years had worn deep mental grooves which played the same depressing songs over and over again.

But then she learned she didn't have to sing along. Christ died on the cross to shatter those records. As that awareness grew, she began to recognize when the tunes started and she replaced them with new songs from God's Word. When people hear the liberating truth that past incidents (whether done by them or to them) need not dictate their present experience, hope springs up in their hearts.

She could say truthfully, "It is no longer *my* past, but *Christ's* past that is now the decisive factor in my life because I am united with him in his death and

---

[21] Mark 7.20-23.
[22] If you were born after 1980, ask an old person what a phonograph needle is.

resurrection!" Rather than being paralyzed by condemnation and discouragement, she was able to turn such memories into occasions to thank God for forgiving her sin and setting her free.

During my years in Lancaster, I knew a godly lady who led a ministry for women with crisis pregnancies. She told me that most of the women became pregnant as a result of sexual sin, but often became believers, receiving Jesus' forgiveness. About five months into their pregnancies, however, when they began to feel the babies move within them, they would be freshly reminded of their former sins and tempted to fall into discouragement.

But this lady taught the young mothers to allow the babies' movements to remind them of God's mercy in forgiving them and to recall that God also promised to cause all things to work together for their good. The quickening of the babies prompted praise to God! *That* was wise counsel indeed!

Through union with Jesus Christ in his death and resurrection, we have died to the penalty and power of sin. His crucified body atoned for our guilt and his resurrected body promises us ultimate victory. Our union with him is the basis for our deliverance from the bondage of sin.

It is as immoveable as it is unmerited; as sufficient as it is certain. If we will but seek to **know** the truth, **consider** it to be so and **present** ourselves in consistent obedience to God, we will move from faith to faith, strength to strength, and glory to glory.

Clashes with Conscience

It's one of my earliest memories. I couldn't have been more than four years old. It was a beautiful Saturday morning, it must have been Saturday because my Dad was not at work. On the window sill in my bedroom sat a rectangular bank made of thick glass. It was filled with coins. Mostly pennies, but a good number of nickels and dimes and even a few quarters could be seen. I think that the only thing I knew about money at that time was that it was desirable. And I desired it. I wanted to handle those coins, not just look at them.

I can't recall what I was thinking beforehand, but it was clearly a pre-meditated crime. Because very quietly I took the bank down, got a hammer and slipped out into the far end of the back yard where a wheelbarrow lay on its side. And there, hidden behind the wheelbarrow, I raised that hammer and smashed that bank.

All the coins poured out mixed with shards of glass. And at that very moment, another kind of hammer came down as my conscience smote me—and I broke. With tears streaming down my face, I ran into the house and confessed to my parents what I had done. Funny, I can't remember anything after that.

* * *

Now it's 1961 and several students are gathered outside the sixth-grade classroom of McKenney Hills Elementary School waiting for the teacher to open the door. I have a rubber band in my hand and I shoot it into the crowd. I didn't expect it to hit anyone in the eye, but it did. And when Jennie screamed out in pain, "My eye! My eye!" neither she nor any of my classmates knew what had happened. But I knew. My conscience also knew and insisted that I take responsibility for what I'd done.

I was scared. What if she was blinded? I tried to argue my case, "It was an accident. It was unintentional," all to no avail. My conscience refused to let me off the hook. The only way to clear it was to admit my guilt and face the consequences. Finally, I spoke to Jennie and the teacher. Thankfully her eye would be okay and she graciously forgave me.

This brings up the most remarkable feature of conscience—the judgments it renders are completely objective and unbiased. In other words, you can never win an argument with your conscience. Its judgments are categorical, unappealable and final.

"You lied." "No, I didn't." "Yes, you did. You told your boss you worked six hours and you only worked three."

"But it was six hours' worth of work squeezed into three. I worked efficiently." "No, you lied." And on and on it goes.

Conscience doesn't actually argue the point, it just states it. It doesn't make any attempt to soften the blow either, such as, "Please sit down. You're a wonderful person but here you fell a bit short." You just can't win against conscience. But that is not to say you can't stifle it, drown it out, cauterize it, deaden it. There's a reason why drugs and alcohol are so popular.

The ancient Greek poets represented the terrors of conscience by *the Furies*, female spirits of justice and vengeance who followed the criminal, tormenting him for his crimes. Cries of conscience are the stuff of which great novels are written, such as Dostoyevsky's *Crime and Punishment*.

What is conscience and where does it come from? The etymology of the word suggests that it is "a knowing together." It's basically a moral awareness of right and wrong.[23] "The human conscience is the subjective proof of humanity's fall, a witness to human guilt before the face of God."[24] In the Old Testament the word "heart" can carry the connotation of conscience. When David dishonored King Saul by surreptitiously cutting off a corner of his robe while Saul was doing his business, we're told that

---

[23] "The conscience is our God-given inner voice, an internal witness that testifies to the level of our personal obedience using God's perfect law as a measuring stick. Its voice is heard in both our mind and our emotions. Sometimes it whispers; sometimes it shouts. Jerry Bridges, *The Bookends of the Christian Life*, Crossway Publishers, Wheaton, 2009, p. 54.

[24] Herman Bavinck, Reformed Dogmatics, Vol. 3, Baker Academic, Grand Rapids, 2006, p. 173.

afterward his heart "smote him" (I Samuel 24.5 KJV). Other translations use the term "conscience-stricken" (NIV; NAS).

In the New Testament the word is used several times. It signifies a man's knowledge of himself as standing in God's presence, subject to his Word and the judgment of his law. *It is self-awareness in the presence of God.*

A clear conscience is one of the most precious benefits of the new birth. It bestows a humble confidence in God and our relationship with him.

> *How much more will the blood of Christ*, who through the eternal Spirit offered himself without blemish to God, *purify our conscience* from dead works to serve the living God.... Since we have confidence to enter the holy places by the blood of Jesus... let us draw near with a true heart in full assurance of faith, with *our hearts sprinkled clean from an evil conscience* and our bodies washed with pure water.[25]

Only the blood of Christ is able to cleanse a conscience stained by sin. It's strange to think of blood as a cleansing agent but that is exactly what the blood of Christ does.

Once having gained a clear conscience, we should do everything we can to maintain it. Since it acts like the warning light on the dashboard of our lives, we need to heed its flashing, determine the source of the difficulty and set about to correct the problem. Usually, the solution involves confessing sin and seeking forgiveness.

Listen to David as he reports how his conscience did its job. As long as he was silent, his conscience was not. But as

---

[25] Hebrews 9.14; 10.19, 22 (emphasis added).

soon as he decided to acknowledge his sin, forgiveness, deliverance and peace came to him.

> *Blessed is the one whose transgression is forgiven,*
> *whose sin is covered.*
> *Blessed is the man against whom the* L*ORD*
> *counts no iniquity*
> *and in whose spirit there is no deceit.*
> *For when I kept silent, my bones wasted away*
> *through my groaning all the day long.*
> *For day and night your hand was heavy upon me;*
> *my strength was dried up as by the heat of summer.*

(Then the change came.)

> *I acknowledged my sin to you,*
> *and I did not cover my iniquity,*
> *I said, 'I will confess my transgressions to the* L*ORD,'*
> *and you forgave the iniquity of my sin.*[26]

By his own admission the apostle Paul was the chief of sinners. Yet he claimed to have a clear conscience before God and men.[27] He encouraged Timothy with regard to conscience:

> This charge I entrust to you, Timothy, my child, in accordance with the prophecies previously made about you, that by them you may wage the good warfare, holding faith and a good conscience. By

---

[26] Psalm 32.1-5.
[27] Cf. Acts 23.1; 24.16.

rejecting these, some have made shipwreck of their faith.[28]

Waging warfare and avoiding shipwreck. Paul seems to be telling Timothy to be both a good soldier and a good sailor. J.B. Phillips' paraphrase captures the imagery well:

> I sent you out to battle for the right armed only with your faith and a clear conscience. Some, alas, have laid these simple weapons contemptuously aside and as far as their faith is concerned, have run their ships on the rocks.[29]

Conscience is a valuable piece of navigational equipment given to help us maneuver through the treacherous waters of this world. But as valuable as conscience is, it is not infallible. It may be unformed or even malformed unless it is informed by the Word of God. Jiminy Cricket's maxim, "Let your conscience be your guide," is only partly wise.

For instance, there is the danger of a seared conscience. I Timothy 4.2 speaks of the insincerity of liars whose consciences are seared, literally cauterized. Where there was once tender flesh now only the scar tissue of seared flesh remains, no longer sensitive to touch.

When I was eighteen someone offered me a joint of marijuana. I knew it was illegal and I knew it was wrong. My conscience was screaming at me. But I did it anyway. A couple of days later I did it again. This time my conscience could still be heard, but more faintly. After a few more times I couldn't hear it at all. This proved to be a

---

[28] I Timothy 1.18-19.
[29] I Timothy 1.18-19 (Phillips Version).

momentous step into a period of misery. When we stifle our conscience we lose the ability to distinguish right from wrong and are in danger of a lee shore, of running our ship on the rocks.

On the other side, there is the problem of an overly scrupulous conscience. For the person with the weak conscience, trifling things can produce fear and anxiety. A trivial act or a heedless word becomes magnified into a barely pardonable sin. An offhand comment not completely accurate morphs into a premeditated lie. Failure to pick up a piece of trash becomes a major offense because "for him who knows the right thing to do, and fails to do it, for him it is sin" (James 4.17). To the person with an overly sensitive conscience the distinction between temptation and sin becomes blurred to the point that perspective is lost and grace nonexistent. This is self-examination run amuck.

I have known conscientious Christians who have tied themselves up in knots because of an overactive conscience. Freedom comes when we regain a view of the grace of God by going back to gospel basics. We are sinners but we have been saved through the grace of our Lord.

To focus on *him*, thanking *him*, worshipping and praising *him* instead of introspectively looking at ourselves is the way forward. Someone has wisely said, for each look at yourself, look ten times to the cross of your merciful Jesus, who died to set you free! It is good for the heart to be strengthened by grace.[30]

---

[30] Hebrews 13.9.

5. *Grace*, Wisdom and the Fear of the LORD

Come, my children, listen to me; I will teach you the fear of the LORD.[1]

Psalm 112

> Praise the LORD!
> Blessed is the man who fears the LORD,
>   who greatly delights in his commandments!
> His offspring will be mighty in the land;
>   the generation of the upright will be blessed.
> Wealth and riches are in his house,
>   and his righteousness endures forever.
> Light dawns in the darkness for the upright;
>   he is gracious, merciful, and righteous.
> It is well with the man who deals generously and lends;
>   who conducts his affairs with justice.
> For the righteous will never be moved;
>   he will be remembered forever.
> He is not afraid of bad news;
>   his heart is firm, trusting in the LORD.
> His heart is steady; he will not be afraid,
>   until he looks in triumph on his adversaries.
> He has distributed freely; he has given to the poor;
>   his righteousness endures forever;
>   his horn is exalted in honor.
> The wicked man sees it and is angry;
>   he gnashes his teeth and melts away;

---

[1] Psalm 34.11 (New International Version).

the desire of the wicked will perish![2]

This is a wisdom psalm, a poem describing the ideal man. This is what we should all aspire to, though we'll never fully reach it. Psalm 112 is for men what Proverbs 31 is for women. And like Proverbs 31 it is an acrostic, each line beginning with the succeeding letter of the Hebrew alphabet. From A to Z, from beginning to end, so to speak, *this* is what the ideal man looks like.

Just as men can benefit from Proverbs 31 women can profit from this psalm. Actually, Psalms 111 and 112 are meant to be read together. The last verse of Psalm 111 and the first of Psalm 112 show the connection between the two:

The fear of the L*ORD* *is the beginning of* ***wisdom****,*
all those who practice it have a good understanding.
His praise endures forever! (Psalm 111.10)

Praise the L*ORD!* ***Blessed*** *is the man who* ***fears the*** L*ORD,*
who greatly delights in his commandments! (Psalm 112.1)

There are three significant themes in this psalm which are also found throughout the Bible's wisdom literature. They are **wisdom**, the **fear of the** L**ORD** and what it means to be **blessed**. Let's look at them more closely.

---

[2] Psalm 112 (ESV).

Wisdom—The Principal Thing

One simple way to define wisdom: *seeing the world as God sees it and acting accordingly*. Because the all-powerful and all-knowing God created and organized the world, he knows how it works. Our power and knowledge are lacking, to say the least. We need God's help to see the world as he sees it so we can align ourselves with his ways. That is what is meant by wisdom.

But it's not so easy. Life's journey takes many unexpected turns. No matter what stage of the voyage we find ourselves in, life is tough. We see this in small children who immediately melt down when things don't go their way.

But it's not only children. The teen-age years, coming of age, single life, married life, raising kids, middle age, old age, the approach of death—they all have their challenges and try us to the very core of our being. I'm sure that If I went back to junior high school *now* I could handle the social awkwardness and peer pressure much better than I did then.

The fact is, wherever we may be in our journey, we find ourselves in tough spots and facing difficult questions. Some of them have huge ramifications, like, "What career shall I pursue?" "Whom shall I marry?" Or perhaps, "Can I find anyone who would marry me?"

All this requires wisdom—how to think and how to act. We desperately need it. And wisdom is not a matter of I.Q. or G.P.A. or S.A.T. It's not knowledge but wisdom that's needed. Wisdom puts knowledge to use properly. Knowledge without wisdom doesn't profit and can be downright dangerous. *Wisdom is the principal thing; therefore get wisdom!*[3]

Where Can Wisdom Be Found?

Where do we find it? Where can we locate the skills we need for navigating the pathways of life? Tucked away in the Book of Job is a fascinating passage. In Chapter 28, the question is asked repeatedly, "Where is wisdom to be found?" And the answers come back:

> It's not found in the land of the living. The realm of death says, "We heard a rumor of it." The deep says, "It's not in me." The sea says, "It's not with me." From where, then does wisdom come? It is hidden from the eyes of all living and concealed from the birds of the air.[4]

Job 28 takes this little survey, "Where can wisdom be found?" And the results come in: "We've canvassed life and death, land, sea and air"—in other words, everything there is— "and we have absolutely no idea!"

But then at the end of the passage come these words: "God understands the way to it and he knows its place... And he said to man, '**Behold, the fear of the Lord,** *that* **is wisdom**...'" (Job 28.23, 28). So! There's a connection, a totally unexpected connection between wisdom and the fear of the LORD.[5]

---

[3] Proverbs 4.7 (KJV).
[4] Job 28.13-14,21-22.
[5] The same correlation may be seen in Proverbs 2.1-8.

The Fear of the LORD

I was about 10 years old when I first heard the expression, "the fear of the LORD." A book I was reading about people living in the 1700s described them as "God-fearing people." I remember my reaction. I didn't like the phrase. There are plenty of things to be afraid of. Please, let's not add God.

A few years later my friend Ed vehemently declared how much he hated that term. "Hah! Fear of God. Should be love of God that people talk about, not fear of God!" Since Ed was an authority on rock and roll, I figured he knew what he was talking about. "Yeah, love of God. I like that better. I think." Pretty common feeling, I suspect. Well, it's just about gone out of use, a vestige of an almost forgotten Puritan past. And I think most people would say, "Good riddance."

Of course, I will argue that the term should not only be revived in our speech, but that the idea it contains should permeate our minds and soak into our hearts. Far from being put off by it, it should fill us with joy and wonder, awe and delight. Because Scripture teaches that:

- The fear of the LORD is the beginning of knowledge.[6]
- The fear of the LORD is the beginning of wisdom.[7]
- And the conclusion of the matter is, fear God and keep his commandments.[8]

---

[6] Proverbs 1.7.
[7] Proverbs 9.10.
[8] Ecclesiastes 12.13.

So, the beginning, the end and everything in between has to do with the fear of the LORD. Besides, there are many other blessings associated with it.

Actually, Ed was getting at something important when he contended for the "love of God" over the "fear of God." But he wrongly assumed the two notions were opposed. They are meant to go together. As Arnold and Beyer argue:

> Important concepts related to keeping covenant are the words, *love* and *fear*, both of which Moses uses repeatedly in Deuteronomy Chapters 6-11. In this unit, Moses urges the Israelites to both love and fear God. These ideas are not incompatible. Rather, they complement and need each other. Love without fear becomes sappy sentimentalism and fails to result in obedience. Likewise, fear without love becomes terror and drives people away from an intimate relationship with God. Together love and fear produce a healthy relationship with Him, and result in obedience to His will.[9]

There is also another difficulty with "the fear of the LORD." The idea can be used in two different senses. First, it can refer to the terror experienced by unrepentant sinners facing the God whose wrath they deserve. Jonathan Edwards had this in mind when he preached his famous sermon, "Sinners in the Hands of an Angry God." Some dismiss Edwards as just an angry man. But he wasn't. Neither was Jesus when he said, even more strongly than Edwards:

---

[9] Bill T. Arnold and Brian E. Beyer, *Encountering the Old Testament*, Baker Books, Grand Rapids, 1999, p. 146.

> I tell you, my friends, do not be afraid of those who kill the body and after that can do no more. But I will show you whom you should fear: Fear him who, after the killing of the body, has power to throw you into hell. Yes, I tell you, fear him.[10]

> Our God is a consuming fire.[11]

> It is a fearful thing to fall into the hands of the living God.[12]

Hard words for modern ears. I can imagine many saying, "That's not the kind of God I believe in." A.W. Tozer wisely wrote, "We can hold a correct view of truth only by daring to believe everything God has said about Himself. It is a grave responsibility that a man takes upon himself when he seeks to edit out of God's self-revelation such features as he in his ignorance deems objectionable."[13]

That *was* a hard saying of Jesus just quoted, but we must remember, Jesus also willingly offered himself on the cross. And why? For the express purpose of saving sinners, like you and me from experiencing such a dreadful destiny.

Fact: You can be forgiven through believing in Jesus. You can be forgiven of all your sins. If you turn away from them and trust in Jesus, God *promises* to forgive you.

> If you confess with your mouth that Jesus is Lord and believe in your heart that God raised him from

---

[10] Luke 12.5 (NIV).
[11] Hebrews 12.29.
[12] Hebrews 10.31.
[13] A.W. Tozer, *The Knowledge of the Holy*, Christian Publications, Harrisburg, 1961.

the dead, you will be saved. For with the heart one believes and is justified, and with the mouth one confesses and is saved.[14]

That's what the Bible says! And when we come to believe in Jesus, the fear of the LORD is transformed into something wonderful. The sense of the term is changed. When the expression "fear of the LORD" is used with respect to the Christian believer, there is a tremendous difference. The dread of final judgment is no longer in view. That's because Jesus himself faced and suffered the terrors of judgment and the penalty for sin as our substitute. The result for us is no rejection, no more fear of torment, and no condemnation by God. Perfect love has cast out fear![15]

The fear of the LORD still has an important place in the life of the believer, however. It is the foundation for our relationship with God. Sinclair Ferguson writes:

> True fear of God almost defies definition, because it is really a synonym for the heartfelt worship of God for who and what He is.... A sense that His opinion about my life is the only thing that really matters. To someone who fears God, His fatherly approval means everything, and the loss of it is the greatest of all griefs. To fear God is to have a heart that is sensitive to both His god-ness and His graciousness.[16]

---

[14] Romans 10.9-10.
[15] I John 4.18; Ephesians 1.6; Romans 8.1.
[16] Sinclair Ferguson, *The Fear of the Lord: Seeing God as He Is*, Discipleship Journal, Archives, Issue 52, 1989, p. 41, resources4discipleship.com.

There is an appropriate and reverent fear and respect we must have toward God. It is warm and filial, our hearts crying to Him, "Abba Father." It is familiar but it is not flippant.

In C.S. Lewis' *The Lion, The Witch and the Wardrobe*, the children are awaiting the arrival of Aslan, who represents Jesus. But when Susan learns that Aslan is a lion, she says, "Ooh! I'd thought he was a man. Is he—quite safe?" Mr. Beaver answered, "Safe? Who said anything about safe? Of course, he's not safe. But he's good. He's the King, I tell you."

He's not tame and he's not safe. But he's good. And the fear of him is the beginning of wisdom!

Blessed!

The first verse of Psalm 112 contains the important word *blessed*. It's often translated happiness, which sort of gets at it. Happiness is the universal human pursuit. Whatever else we may say we're after, it is still but a means to gain happiness.

Blessed means more than happiness, however. It means to be blissfully happy over the long haul—a constant state of well-being, contentment and satisfaction. Not momentary, fleeting pleasure, but enduring well-being. Sort of like Christmas morning *every* morning.

For me, the happiest day of the year was not Christmas morning but the last day of school. No more writing, no more books, no more teacher's dirty looks! That last day of school meant the first day of summer, an endless summer of freedom and fun! That is, until school started again.

* * *

The biblical idea of blessedness is connected with holiness. That means not only that God is involved in it but God is the *focus* of it! Blessedness is total joy in the presence of a completely loving and accepting God.[17]

> (a) Blessed is the man who **fears the Lord**,
> (b) who **greatly delights in his commandments!**
> (Psalm 112.1)

The first verse is the key to the entire psalm. This is poetry and the chief characteristic of Hebrew poetry is called *parallelism*. The second line (b) is parallel to the first line (a). They correspond with each other. So, the blessed man who **fears the Lord** in line (a) is further explained by line (b). He is the man who **greatly delights in the Lord's commandments**.

This is intended to grab our attention. We don't associate fear with delight, much less great delight. But that is exactly the point we are to get. There is something about God's Word that is delightful. And it's connected to the fear of the Lord. It's not apparent at first. But if you stop and think about it, it makes sense. The commandments of the Lord are his words, the Bible. It is the instruction that brings wisdom which in turn brings life. If we fear the Lord we will delight in His words, even *greatly* delight in them.

---

[17] I heard of a survey conducted a few years ago among celebrities. The question was asked whether they believed in heaven. Almost all did. And then a second question, whether they believed they would go there upon death. Almost all believed that, too. But when asked to describe heaven, no one mentioned God being there.

Have you ever noticed how often the psalmists rhapsodize over God's words? This is especially seen in Psalms 19 and 119. Are they just being effusive? No, they are being wise! The blessed man of Psalm 112 loves God's words, too. He is the wise man who fears the LORD.

The man who fears the LORD is the man who greatly delights in his Word. This is the man who will be blessed. And *this* is the key point. If this is operative in our lives, if we truly love God's Word, all the rest that is in this psalm will inevitably follow. It will be ours, perhaps not immediately, but eventually it will *surely* be ours. What follows verse 1 is a laundry list of marvelous blessings.

1. Blessed Family

> His offspring (descendants) will be mighty in the land;
> the generation of the upright will be blessed. (2)

If you fear the LORD, and greatly delight in his commandments, your descendants will benefit. They will be mighty in the land. They will make a difference. They will be significant. They will contribute to church and society. That is the promise here. And they themselves will be blessed. The overwhelming number of people who become Christians are those who were raised in homes where fathers and mothers have been genuine believers, fearing God and loving his Word.

2. Blessed Wealth

> Wealth and riches are in his house,
> and his righteousness endures forever. (3)

This is not a promise of luxury. In an agrarian culture of subsistence farmers, wealth meant having a good harvest. It meant you had food for your own household and enough left over to give to those in need. By this standard almost all of us today would be considered fabulously wealthy.

This man's blessed wealth is matched by his generosity. He is not a miser. He's not a hoarder, he's a giver. He deals generously and lends (v. 5). He distributes freely; he gives to the poor (v. 9). He's generous, merciful and righteous (v. 4).

3. Blessed Stability

> Light dawns in the **darkness** for the upright; (4a)
> For the righteous will never be moved (6a)
> He is not afraid of **bad news**;
> > his heart is firm, trusting in the Lord. (7)
> His heart is steady; he will not be **afraid**,
> > until he looks in triumph on his **adversaries**. (8)

There *is* darkness, there *is* bad news, there *are* things to fear and there *are* adversaries.
This is real life. We are not in heaven yet. Bad news comes and bad things happen. But for this man, light arises in the darkness. Weeping may indeed last for the night, but joy comes in the morning.[18]

This man is not afraid of bad news. His heart is firm; his heart is steady; it is fixed and established. Why? One little phrase at the end of verse 7 says it all. He actively and constantly *trusts in the* Lord, the covenant keeping God

---

[18] Psalm 30.5.

whose promises never fail. This is what characterizes his life. To trust in the LORD is to fear the LORD.

The fundamental question for each of us at every step along the way is this: Am I trusting the LORD? If so, my life will not be characterized by craven fear. This doesn't mean there won't be times when we stumble. We all do. Even the righteous man falls seven times, but he rises again.[19] The basic tenor of our lives will be a quiet confidence and trust in God.

In more than forty years of pastoral ministry, I have seen some difficult times, personally and as a church leader. People have sometimes commented, "You seem so even-keeled, so stable." To whatever extent that may be true, it's not due to having a certain personality type, but to knowing a faithful God. I have had many sleepless nights of prayer, fighting for faith, meditating on Scripture. In other words, I've had to work at it. We are to work out our salvation in fear and trembling. But we can do so knowing God is at work in us both to will and to work for his good pleasure.[20] "God is our refuge and strength, a very present help in trouble."[21] His faithfulness never fails.

4. Blessed Memory

This doesn't mean he won't misplace his car keys or forget why he walked into a room. It's not his memory, but others' memory of him.

---

[19] Proverbs 24.16.
[20] Philippians 2.12-13.
[21] Psalm 46.1.

He will be remembered forever. (6a)
His righteousness endures forever; (9b)
His horn is exalted in honor. (9c)

He will be remembered. And it will be a pleasant memory. When a president leaves office there is usually talk of his legacy. What mark has he made; what will he be remembered for? What about you and me? What will we be leaving behind? What will people think when they think of us? Will they think of us at all? As people grow older they wonder about these things.

I started this book with a question: how much do you remember about your parents and grandparents? After a few generations the memory of them fades away. It would be nice to be remembered by my descendants, I admit. But what is much more important is to be remembered by my LORD. The man who fears the LORD... will be remembered forever.

There is an amazing statement in Malachi:

> Then those who feared the LORD spoke with one another. The LORD paid attention and heard them, and a book of remembrance was written before him of those who feared the LORD and esteemed his name. "They shall be mine, says the LORD of hosts, in the day when I make up my treasured possession, and I will spare them as a man spares his son who serves him."[22]

---

[22] Malachi 3.16-17.

The book of Malachi is structured around a number of disputations that God has with his people who have been critical, disobedient and even cynical. Most of them are not in a good place. But then he addresses another group with which he is pleased. What characterizes this group is *the fear of the* LORD.

Those who feared the LORD *spoke with one another.* That sounds like fellowship, that sounds like the church, the community of like-minded, God-fearing people. *The* LORD *paid attention and heard them.* God is paying attention to our conversations. That's a sobering thought. What is the general drift of your words? Would God be pleased with what he hears? *And a book of remembrance was written before him with the names of those who feared him and esteemed his name.* This must be the book of life. Jesus encouraged his disciples to rejoice that their names are written in heaven. *They shall be mine... in the day when I make up my treasured possession.* In ancient times, a king had access to all the wealth in his realm. But in addition, he would also have a personal treasure, his private stash, consisting of the most precious jewels and other valuables. In the same way, those who fear the LORD are special to him.

Nobody wants to be forgotten. Those who fear the LORD will be remembered in the most important way. They trust in Him with all their heart. Thus shall the man be blessed who fears the LORD!

One final question. If all Scripture finds its fulfillment in Jesus Christ,[23] where is he in all this? Well, Jesus *is* the blessed man of Psalm 112. He is the ideal man. He is what every man and every woman was meant to be. He is

---

[23] Luke 24.27, 44.

generous, righteous, strong and stable. Jesus' relationship with his heavenly Father perfectly demonstrates the fear of the Lord. He himself is our wisdom,[24] in him are found all the treasures of wisdom and knowledge.[25] To know him is life eternal. To know him is to be truly wise. And the wise still seek him.

---

[24] I Corinthians 1.30.
[25] Colossians 2.3.

6: *Gratitude* for a Grand Inheritance!

*A good man leaves an inheritance
to his children's children….*[1]

I would love to leave something of material benefit to my grandchildren. Of far greater value is the spiritual inheritance that belongs to all God's children.

In an earlier chapter, we considered the great blessing of justification. The imagery surrounding this doctrine comes straight from the law court. God who is the Lawgiver and Judge of all the earth issued a declaration that acquits the condemned sinner because of his faith in Jesus Christ. Justification gives us a brand-new status before God, exonerating us from all sin and the penalties associated with it. Though we were convicted felons awaiting the inevitable on death row, the Judge pardoned us and expunged our criminal records.[2] But as wonderful as this is, there is an aspect of justification even more remarkable.

I've been in a few courtrooms and they are not very cheerful places. You can't relax, put your feet up or laugh out loud. You wouldn't think of yukking it up with the judge during the trial. There is a certain decorum, formal and intimidating which is in keeping with the business that goes on there. It's meant to be that way. It's no less true in the presence of God as sovereign Judge.

---

[1] Proverbs 13.22.
[2] Colossians 2.13-14.

But for the Christian there is a monumental difference between heaven's courtroom and its earthly counterpart. Because after decreeing us free from all condemnation, the Judge does not retreat to his chambers. Instead he steps down from the bench, gathers the forgiven into his arms and carries them from the courtroom to the family room.

This is known as the doctrine of adoption. It is a part of justification as God becomes our Father and we his children. The Scriptures make it clear that we are legally and intimately related to God as his children! Not only is this true, but to be his child carries many privileges. Paul described it like this: "The Spirit himself bears witness with our spirit that we are children of God, and if children, then heirs—heirs of God and fellow heirs with Christ, provided we suffer with him in order that we may also be glorified with him."[3]

While justification and adoption come to us as free gifts, we should always remember the infinite price that was paid to secure them, for it cost the Father his Son and it cost the Son his life. The cost to us is our pride, for the only way to receive this gift is to come to God in humility and repentant faith.

Children of God. Heirs of God. Fellow heirs with Christ. That is what we are. What does it all mean? Let us first establish a crucial fact. Jesus Christ, God's only begotten Son is the Father's true and rightful heir. Any inheritance we have is ours only because we are "in Christ."[4]

---

[3] Romans 8.16-17.
[4] Ephesians 1.11; 2.7.

Furthermore, Christ himself embodies this inheritance. *He* is our peace, *he* is our righteousness, our hope, our sanctification, our redemption. *In him* are hidden all the treasures of wisdom and knowledge. *He* is the resurrection and the life. The greatest gift we will ever receive from God is Jesus Christ himself.

It is important to remember that this inheritance comes not through a doctrine but through a Person. The doctrine is there to help us understand the Person and what he has done. Doctrinal knowledge is not to be disparaged, as though there is some sort of disconnect between the Person and the truth about the Person. There is not. Nevertheless, it is possible to have a certain level of knowledge about God without a corresponding heart commitment to the God who is revealed. "Did not our hearts burn within us... as he opened to us the Scriptures?"[5]

Peace with God—Reconciliation

> Therefore, since we have been justified by faith, we have peace with God through our Lord Jesus Christ.... For if while we were enemies we were reconciled to God by the death of his Son, much more, now that we are reconciled shall we be saved by his life. More than that, we also rejoice in God through our Lord Jesus Christ, through whom we have now received reconciliation.[6]

When surveying something as vast and wonderful as our spiritual inheritance, it's hard to know where to begin.

---

[5] Luke 24.32.
[6] Romans 5.1, 10-11.

Writing here about the results of justification, Paul first mentions peace with God. This underlies everything else we receive in Christ. It is the gift that puts all the other blessings in perspective.

"The primary business of the Christian gospel is not to give us blessings," wrote David Martyn Lloyd-Jones. "Its primary business is to reconcile us to God."[7] While there is a subjective peace *of* God (that is, one that may be felt), what Paul has in mind here is peace *with* God, the objective fact that the gospel has removed every obstacle that separated us from him.

To reconcile means to bring together parties divided because of hostility. When Stephen was arraigned before the council in Jerusalem, he recounted an incident from the life of Moses.

> And on the following day he appeared to them (two Israelites) as they were quarreling and tried to reconcile them, saying, "Men, you are brothers. Why do you wrong each other?"[8]

The King James version of the Bible translates "reconcile" as "set them at one again." The phrase in Greek includes the word normally translated "peace." What we must grasp is that from God's point of view there is no more hostility between him and those he has justified. His wrath against sin was righteously expressed and fully satisfied at the cross. Now, the battle is over. We've been set at one with God. Reconciliation has taken place and we have peace with God.

---

[7] D. Martyn Lloyd-Jones, *Romans: Assurance, Chapter Five*, Zondervan Publishing House, Grand Rapids, 1971, p. 10.
[8] Acts 7.26.

Not only has the conflict been resolved but any legal problems resulting from former hostilities have been erased, never to reappear. "There is therefore now no condemnation for those who are in Christ Jesus.... Who shall bring any charge against God's elect? It is God who justifies."[9] If the highest court in the universe has declared us justified, there is not a charge that can stick.

But "no condemnation" does *not* mean "no accusation." There is an enemy who continues the dirty work of casting aspersions and shooting fiery darts. And it often happens that we mistake God's gifts of conviction and correction for the devil's denunciations.

The fact that Jesus has taken our place as substitute for our sins means that we shall never face the condemnation of final judgement. "Who is to condemn? Christ Jesus is the one who died—more than that, who was raised—who is at the right hand of God, who indeed is interceding for us."[10]

> When our holy war with God ceases, when we like Luther walk through the doors of Paradise, when we are justified by faith, the war ends forever. With the cleansing from sin and the declaration of divine forgiveness we enter into a peace treaty with God that is eternal. The first fruit of our justification is peace with God. This peace is a holy peace, a peace unblemished and transcendent. It is a peace that cannot be destroyed.[11]

---

[9] Romans 8.1, 33.
[10] Romans 8.34.
[11] R.C. Sproul, *The Holiness of God*, Tyndale House Publishers, Wheaton, 1985, p. 193. While writing these lines I learned that Dr. Sproul had died. He now knows that Paradise first hand. What a gift he has been to the church!

Knowing that we have peace with God puts our minds at rest. It enables us to overcome worries and fears. Even if the whole world were to oppose us, we remain secure in Christ. God, who is worthy of our fear, has initiated an eternal pact of peace with us. For the Christian established in this truth, even the fear of death is vanquished because the threat of judgment no longer exists.

Forgiveness of Sin

Closely related to reconciliation and peace with God is forgiveness of sin. Is this precious truth in danger of being despised? When people lament and say, "I know I'm forgiven but…." I can't help wondering, "But *do* you know you are forgiven? If you really understood forgiveness whatever problem you have wouldn't seem nearly so bad." As Lloyd-Jones implies above, man's greatest need is forgiveness, deliverance from sin. And if God has forgiven us, any other problem is minor by comparison.

It is rare today to hear Christians rejoice in being forgiven by God. I suppose this is understandable in a culture that still views low self-esteem as a greater concern than alienation from God.

Our awareness of forgiveness determines our affection for God. That was the gist of Jesus' response to the self-righteous Pharisee, Simon. "He who has been forgiven little, loves little," Jesus told him.[12] Conversely, he who has been forgiven much, loves much. The truth is, we are all in the second category. Consider the following:

---

[12] Luke 7.47.

- Pardon for sin comes to us only on the basis of Jesus' shed blood. "In him we have redemption through his blood, the forgiveness of our trespasses, according to the riches of his grace."[13]

- God's motive in forgiveness is his great love. His forgiveness is free and merciful. "God exalted him at his right hand as Leader and Savior, to give repentance to Israel and forgiveness of sins."[14]

- Forgiveness of sins leads to a knowledge of salvation. Jesus came "to give his people the knowledge of salvation through the forgiveness of their sins."[15]

- God's forgiveness is thorough. "I, even I, am he who blots out your transgressions, for my own sake, and remembers your sins no more."[16]

- Understanding forgiveness leads to a right fear of God. "If you, O LORD, should mark iniquities, O Lord, who could stand? But with you there is forgiveness, that you may be feared."[17]

John Owen, perhaps the greatest of the English Puritan theologians, wrote a treatise in the 17th Century on forgiveness from Psalm 130 that still stands as a classic. The

---

[13] Ephesians 1.7.
[14] Acts 5.31.
[15] Luke 1.77.
[16] Isaiah 43.25.
[17] Psalm 130.3-4.

editor's preface provides some insight into the circumstances surrounding the work. It seems that as a young man Owen's awareness of forgiveness was superficial, "until the Lord was pleased to visit me with a sore affliction, whereby I was brought to the mouth of the grave, and under which my soul was oppressed with horror and darkness; but God graciously relieved my spirit by a powerful application of Psalm 130.4 from whence I received special instruction, peace and comfort, in drawing near to God through the Mediator and preached thereupon immediately after my recovery."[18]

Psalm 130.4, as we saw above, shows that fearing the Lord is the natural outgrowth of embracing his forgiveness. While we're young and healthy other problems can seem so much more important. But when we draw near to eternity, knowing whether or not we are forgiven makes all other matters pale into insignificance.

Pardon for sin and a peace that endureth,
Thy own dear presence to cheer and to guide;
Strength for today and bright hope for tomorrow,
Blessings all mine, with ten thousand beside![19]

---

[18] John Owen, *Works, Volume VI*, Banner of Truth Trust, Carlisle, 1967, p. 324.
[19] T.O. Chisholm, *Great is Thy Faithfulness*, Tabernacle Publishing Co., Chicago, 1953, p. 76.

Future inheritance—The Hope of the Resurrection

Peggy Noonan wrote speeches for President Ronald Reagan. In a piece for the 75th anniversary issue of Fortune Magazine she posed the question, "Why do we feel so bad when we have it so good?"

I think we have lost the old knowledge that happiness is overrated, that in a way life is overrated. We have lost somehow a sense of mystery about us, our purpose, our meaning, our role. Our ancestors believed in two worlds and understood this to be the solitary, poor, nasty, brutish and short one. We are the first generation of man that actually expected to find happiness here on earth. And our search for it has left us so unhappy.... The reason for this unhappiness? If you do not believe in another higher world, if you believe only in the flat, material world around you, if you believe that this is your only chance at happiness, then you are not disappointed when this world does not give a good measure of its riches, you are despairing!

Groaning Inwardly and Waiting Eagerly

> But when the fullness of time had come, God sent forth his Son, born of woman, born under the law, to redeem those who were under the law so <u>that we might receive adoption as sons. And because you are sons</u>, God has sent the Spirit of his Son into our hearts, crying, "Abba! Father!" So you are no longer a slave, but a son, and if a son, then an heir through God.[20]

---

[20] Galatians 4.4-7 (emphasis added).

> For I consider that the sufferings of this present time are not worth comparing with the glory that is to be revealed to us. For the creation waits with eager longing for the revealing of the sons of God. For the creation was subjected to futility, not willingly, but because of him who subjected it, in hope that the creation itself will be set free from its bondage to decay and obtain the freedom of the glory of the children of God. For we know that the whole creation has been groaning together in the pains of childbirth until now. And not only the creation, but we ourselves, who have the firstfruits of the Spirit, groan inwardly as <u>we wait eagerly for adoption as sons</u>, <u>the redemption of our bodies</u>. For in this hope we were saved. Now hope that is seen is not hope. For who hopes for what he sees? But if we hope for what we do not see, we wait for it with patience.[21]

These two statements by Paul show that our status as adopted children is both present and future. The future aspect has to do with the redemption of our bodies which will take place at the time of the general resurrection when Christ returns in glory.[22]

Paul places that future glory on a balance opposite the sufferings of this present age and concludes there is simply no comparison. He's not minimizing present sufferings which he knew could be quite severe. But from the perspective of eternity, the glory (which in another place he calls "an eternal weight of glory beyond all comparison"[23]) *far* outweighs the suffering.

---

[21] Romans 8.18-25 (emphasis added).
[22] Cf. I Corinthians 15.50-57; Luke 9.26.
[23] II Corinthians 4.17.

What would cause him to make such a strong and categorical statement? There may be a clue in the unusual personal testimony he presents in II Corinthians 12. In this letter Paul has been patiently reasoning with his spiritually immature children, the Corinthians. They have been despising him because he wasn't as outwardly impressive as some other supposed ministers. Since the Corinthians are enthralled by things like dreams and visions, Paul reluctantly resorts to the same sort of "boasting" in order to make his point.

> I must go on boasting. Though there is nothing to be gained by it. I will go on to visions and revelations of the Lord. I know a man in Christ who fourteen years ago was caught up to the third heaven—whether in the body or out of the body I do not know, God knows. And I know that this man was caught up into paradise—whether in the body or out of the body I do not know, God knows—and he heard things that cannot be told, which man may not utter. On behalf of this man I will boast, but on my own behalf I will not boast, except of my weaknesses. Though if I should wish to boast, I would not be a fool, for I would be speaking the truth. But I refrain from it, so that no one may think more of me than he sees in me or hears from me. So to keep me from being too elated by the surpassing greatness of the revelations, a thorn was given me in the flesh, a messenger of Satan to harass me, to keep me from being too elated.[24]

Of course, the man Paul is referring to here is himself. He employs these circumlocutions because he is uncomfortable drawing unnecessary attention to himself. He does

---

[24] II Corinthians 12.1-7.

not tell us the content of the visions and revelations, but what we can determine from this is that he was privy to knowledge—things he heard and saw—that he was not allowed and perhaps not even able to disclose.

Knowledge of things that were of such surpassing greatness that he was given a thorn in the flesh to keep him from being too elated. He says this twice. *Too elated*!? What did he see? What did he hear? We aren't told. Neither are we told what his thorn was, except that as a messenger from Satan, it harassed and weakened him.

What did Paul witness when he was caught up to the third heaven? Perhaps something so wonderful that the very real sufferings of this present age would appear as nothing by comparison? We know that "in the coming ages, God will show us the immeasurable riches of his grace in kindness toward us in Christ Jesus."[25] But even this lavish language can easily fall on dull ears, and hearts heavy due to the cares of life in a fallen world. After all, the whole creation currently subjected to futility is groaning under a weight of bondage and decay. And not only the creation but we ourselves, who have the firstfruits of the Spirit, also groan.

I'm in my late sixties now, and I am increasingly aware of diminished health and vitality. Noises now emerge from me that could be described as groanings, I suppose. I used to drive a golf ball 260 yards with persimmon woods. Now, even with the new technology, it's 225 tops. What a wretched man I am!

But in this present age our bodies are not for us to glory in, anyway. They are intended to humble us so that we will seek God. Their destiny is to be transformed by Jesus to be

---

[25] Ephesians 2.7.

like his glorious body.[26] *That* is what we are to look forward to.

In the meantime, like the rest of creation that has been groaning as if in the pains of childbirth, we are to eagerly await our adoption as children—the redemption of our bodies. The image of childbirth is apropos. Labor travail is real pain, but pain with a purpose. Sorrow turns into great joy with the emergence of new life![27] Paul says that it was in this hope we were saved (Romans 8.24). But I wonder how many of us think much about the future redemption of our bodies. You should. And the older you get, you will.

It's good to know that the Holy Spirit is there to help us in our weakness, interceding for us with his own groanings too deep for words.[28] So, creation groans, we groan, the Spirit groans. That's a lot of groaning! Praise God that the glory one day revealed will so overwhelm our present sufferings that they will seem like nothing by comparison.

---

[26] Philippians 3.21.
[27] John 16.21.
[28] Romans 8.26.

One More Thing

For the promise to Abraham and his offspring that he would be heir of the world….[1]

Wait! What was that? Heir of the world? Yes. Somehow the promise made to Abraham in Genesis has morphed, in Paul's understanding, to now embrace the entire world, not just Canaan. Abraham's offspring refers ultimately to Christ who will one day exercise an unopposed universal dominion.[2]

But we who are in Christ are also Abraham's offspring and heirs according to the promise.[3] That means that *we* are heirs of the world. It all belongs to *us*. But God, as a good Father, wisely manages it for us. From our inheritance, he doles out to us what we need, when we need it. He knows what is best. He would not wish to ruin us by giving us too much too quickly. After all, it takes a steady hand to hold a full cup. But a day is coming….

Dear brothers and sisters, take heart. Though our immediate situation may be filled with trials and suffering, our long-term prospects are excellent.

---

[1] Romans 4.13.
[2] John R.W. Stott, *Romans*, IVP, Downers Grove, 1994, p. 130.
[3] Galatians 3.29.

And Glory!

When we think of the great acts of the Triune God, the wonderful gospel message immediately comes to mind. God has acted to reconcile fallen and rebellious people to himself at the cost of Jesus' priceless blood. But why has he done this? Certainly, for the benefit of men and women— no greater blessing can be imagined from our viewpoint. But as wonderful as this is, the gospel of reconciliation is ultimately for something more wonderful still—the praise of the glory of God's grace, the honor of his name.

So, there is a fourth G—Glory, God's glory. Jonathan Edwards understood this to be the end for which God created the world, the reason why we and everything else exists. What is our chief end, our *raison d'être*? It is to glorify God and enjoy him forever.

"Glory" is one of those words so common in our Christian vocabulary that we use it assuming we all know what we're talking about. But it is very difficult to define— much used and little understood. If God's glory is his ultimate goal, it is important to try to comprehend it, even if but a little. One place to begin is with creation. Psalm 19 begins with the assertion:

> The heavens declare the glory of God,
> > and the sky above proclaims his handiwork.
> Day to day pours out speech,
> > and night to night reveals knowledge.[4]

---

[4] Psalm 19.1-2.

Both the night sky and the day sky are shouting all the time. They declare and proclaim and pour out speech. And what are they saying? That God *is* and that God is *glorious*. In the verses that follow the psalmist calls on the sun as a star witness (pun intended) to bear testimony not to himself but to God's glory.

And the sun does have a certain glory. It dominates our world like nothing else. All life on earth depends on it. Try staring at it and you'll be quickly overwhelmed. *That* is glory. Now consider that our sun is but a medium-sized star. There are billions more stars of greater size and magnitude. They are even more glorious. And God created them! All of them! How glorious then must God be!

John Frame notes that although God is essentially invisible there are ways he makes himself evident. "Glory is God's visible presence among people."[5] When the tabernacle and the temple were dedicated, God's glorious presence was so great that Moses and the priests were overwhelmed.[6]

---

[5] John Frame, *Systematic Theology*, P&R Publishing, Phillipsburg, 2009, p. 1009.

[6] Exodus 40.34-35; 2 Chronicles 7.1-3. Moses' famous request of God, "Please show me your glory," was met by a revelation of the proclamation of God's *name*: "The LORD, the LORD, a God merciful and gracious, slow to anger and abounding in steadfast love and faithfulness, keeping steadfast love for thousands, forgiving iniquity and transgression and sin, but who will by no means clear the guilty, visiting the iniquity of the fathers on the children and the children's children, to the third and the fourth generation." This revelation reappears and is developed throughout Scripture finding fullest expression in the life and ministry of our Lord Jesus Christ. (Exodus 33.18; 34.5-7)

With the incarnation of Christ, John tells us, "And the Word became flesh and dwelt among us, and we have seen his glory, glory as of the only Son from the Father, full of grace and truth."[7] He turned the water into wine "and manifested his glory," at the wedding feast.[8] He did other signs such as calming the winds and waves with a mere word, leaving his disciples awestruck. "What manner of man is this, that even the wind and the sea obey him?"[9]

And nothing better displayed his glory than the transfiguration when his face shone like the sun and his clothes became as white as light.[10] But that was a momentary unveiling and the disciples were told to keep it secret until he was raised.

Glory in Humiliation

It remains the case that Christ came first in humiliation and not with demonstrated exaltation. Though the angels testified to his glory, Jesus was born as a helpless baby.[11] And it was as a suffering servant that he gave his life as a ransom for many.[12] The Godhead was veiled in flesh.

When Jesus said, "The hour has come for the Son of Man to be glorified,"[13] he was referring to his rapidly approaching death by crucifixion. The night before the cross he prayed, "Father, the hour has come, glorify your Son that

---

[7] John 1.14.
[8] John 2.11.
[9] Mark 4.41 (KJV).
[10] Matthew 17.2.
[11] Luke 2.11-14.
[12] Mark 10.45.
[13] John 12.23.

the Son may glorify you."[14] At the cross the supreme act of sacrificial love resulted in glory for the Father and for his Son, in the Holy Spirit. This was an unexpected kind of glory.

The idea of a crucified Messiah was offensive to the Jews and ridiculous to the Gentiles.[15] But it was the very wisdom of God because after crucifixion came resurrection. In the most dramatic reversal imaginable, God raised his Son from the depths of humiliation to the place of highest honor.[16]

Of course, not everybody sees this. During this present age, Christ's glory can only be seen by the eyes of faith. But a day is coming when every eye shall see him. "For as the lightning flashes and lights up the sky from one side to the other, so will the Son of Man be in his day."[17] At that time every knee shall bow and every tongue confess that Jesus Christ is Lord, to the glory of God the Father.[18] Till then we await our blessed hope, the appearing of the glory of our great God and Savior Jesus Christ.[19]

It is not just Christian believers who await this great day of the Lord. The whole creation waits with eager longing for the revealing of the sons of God, the glory of the children of God, which will occur at the time of Christ's return. We ourselves will participate in that glory as our bodies of humiliation are transformed and made like his glorious body.[20] "And the glory of the LORD shall be revealed, and all

---

[14] John 17.1.
[15] I Corinthians 1.23.
[16] Philippians 2.6-11.
[17] Luke 17.24. Cf. Revelation 1.7.
[18] Philippians 2.10-11.
[19] Titus 2.13.
[20] Cf. Romans 8.19-23; Philippians 3.20-21.

flesh shall see it together, for the mouth of the LORD has spoken it."[21]

This is where things are headed—God's glory. True wisdom is to know this and to fall in line with it. It is the key to life in the midst of this crooked and twisted world.

But can you feel the dilemma? I met recently with an old friend dying of cancer who knows these truths. She was delighted with her own prospects, but her heart was heavy for family and friends. Her only care was for those in her life who did not know him.

You believe in God. You know he is real. You know how wonderful he is. You are trying to represent him to others by the way you live and the words you say. And you *want* them to know him. It breaks your heart that though everyone in the world was created by him, most ignore him. People that you love and work with are living in darkness. You can feel so powerless. You want them to see his glory, his reality!

This is the mission that Jesus has left to us. And it will succeed. We are to go into all the world to make disciples. Finding them and folding them, guarding the gospel and proclaiming the gospel. And all for the glory of God.[22]

God's will is his glory. Therefore it will surely come to pass. As the prophet Habakkuk wrote:

---

[21] Isaiah 40.5.
[22] The glory of God is the material principle of Reformed Theology, i.e. it's central teaching. This way of seeing the Bible and the world rightly sets the glory of God as the goal of our lives and worship. Cf. Q. 1 of the Westminster Shorter Catechism, "What is the chief end of man?" "Man's chief end is to glorify God and enjoy Him forever."

For the earth will be filled with the knowledge of the glory of the LORD as the waters cover the sea.[23]

Not as the waters cover the earth, but as the waters cover the sea, in other words, completely!

Let us rejoice in hope of the glory of God.[24]

Soli Deo Gloria!

---

[23] Habakkuk 2.14.
[24] Romans 5.2.

Twinsies!
(snoring like Pop Pop)

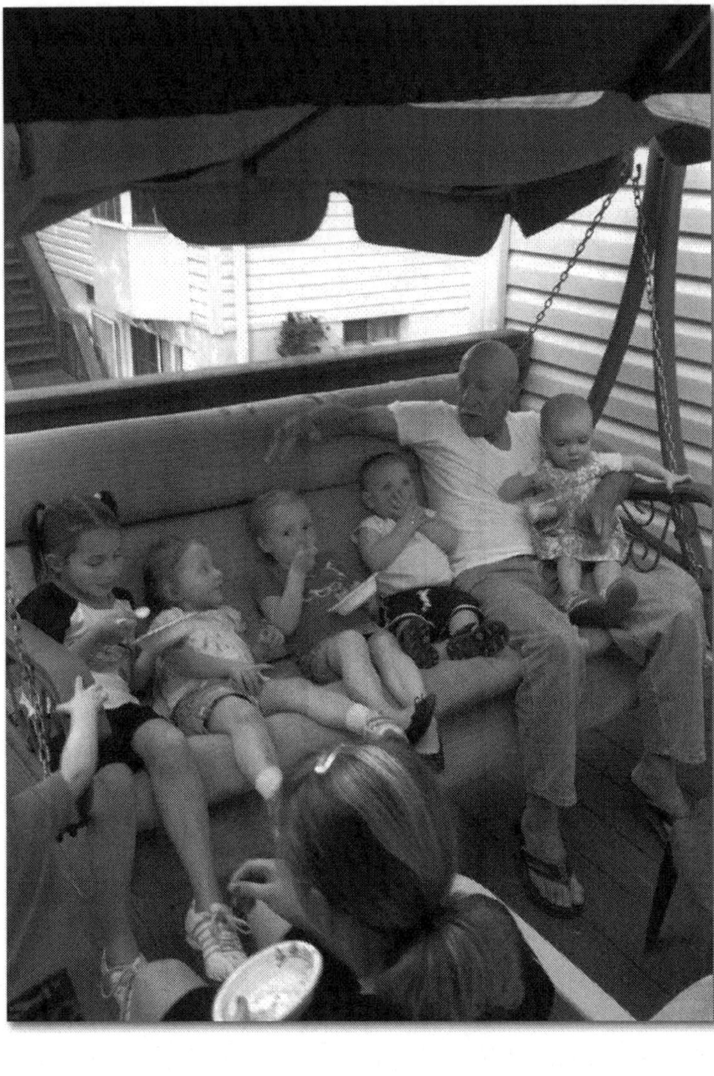

My Dear Grandchildren,

Congratulations! You've made it to the end, not only reading the stories but the material I consider to be most important—about God and His ways with us. I commend you for this. But I have some advice and a challenge for you. <u>Keep learning about the Father, the Son and the Holy Spirit!</u> Acquire knowledge about Him. Get to know Him with your heart and your mind, because as you do, your love for Him will grow and your service for Him will be more effective.

But this won't be easy. C.S. Lewis said, "The only people who achieve much are those who want knowledge so badly that they seek it while the conditions are still unfavorable. Favorable conditions never come."

You've all seen my library. A few thousand volumes, hardly any of which have pictures! I assembled this over a lifetime of pastoral ministry. J.C. Ryle was certainly correct when he wrote, "Tis a melancholy thing what becomes of good men's libraries. Nothing is so cherished by some and despised and neglected by others as books, specially theological books." It would give me great joy to see you walking in the truth. If some of my books might fall into your hands and be used by you to know and love and serve God, that would be icing on my cake!

But whether or not that happens, I urge you to develop a taste for reading sound theology, especially the Christian classics.[1] *There is a reason why they are still around. I have read and reread Augustine's Confessions many times. Other writers worth your energy are Calvin (don't believe the negative comments about him), Herman Bavinck (how I honor the man!) and B.B. Warfield. More contemporary is C.S. Lewis, of course, but also John Murray, J.I. Packer, John R.W. Stott, R.C. Sproul, Sinclair Ferguson, Donald Carson, John Frame, Bruce Waltke and John Piper.*

Of course, there are many others I could name. But that's my starter list for you to consider. Above all, never leave off the reading of Scripture (Psalm 119.97-105). <u>*Keep learning about God!*</u>

Love,

Pop Pop

---

[1] Mark Twain defined a classic as a book everyone wants to have read, but no one wants to read. It's true. But press through this barrier. You'll be glad you did.

Robin Boisvert, a pastor since 1976, has served churches in Washington, D.C., Lancaster, PA and Gaithersburg, MD. He is a graduate of Geneva College, The Center for Urban Theological Studies (Philadelphia) and Reformed Theological Seminary. Robin and Clara have four children and fourteen grandchildren (and counting).

Robin and Clara – 1991

A Full Quiver

Made in the USA
Middletown, DE
04 August 2018